KALAM

KALAM

THE UNTOLD STORY

R.K. PRASAD

BLOOMSBURY

NEW DELHI • LONDON • OXFORD • NEW YORK • SYDNEY

BLOOMSBURY INDIA
Bloomsbury Publishing India Pvt. Ltd
Second Floor, LSC Building No. 4, DDA Complex, Pocket C – 6 & 7,
Vasant Kunj, New Delhi, 110070

BLOOMSBURY, BLOOMSBURY INDIA and the Diana logo
are trademarks of Bloomsbury Publishing Plc

First published in India 2022
This edition published 2022

ISBN: PB: 978-93-54359-72-9, E-book: 978-93-54359-88-0
2 4 6 8 10 9 7 5 3 1

Printed and bound in India by Replika Press Pvt. Ltd.

To my family
for their steady support
through the decades

Contents

Foreword

It had been a long, very hard haul. Work, after extensive discussions, had begun a year earlier on the book *India 2020: A Vision for the New Millennium*, and the authors, A.P.J. Abdul Kalam and Y.S. Rajan, who was also a close friend of his, had submitted it chapter by chapter, each chapter giving facts, figures and projections on how India had the potential to grow and excel in a particular area. The areas ranged from technology to agriculture to healthcare. The book was set on a very tight deadline for release – August 1998, to coincide with Independence Day celebrations. Additionally, the Pokhran-II nuclear tests had happened on 11 and 13 May, in which Dr Kalam had played a prominent role as coordinator.

As India headed towards the new millennium it was the right time to hope for a book that set out a dramatic shift in growth path, taking it from a potential achiever to a top performer. Today India's status as one of the world's biggest economies seems a given, but at the time, as it coped with the sanctions imposed after the nuclear tests besides its own struggling economy, it seemed something far off.

It was not so clear then that the book would make such an impact, virtually setting the agenda for the next twenty years, offering hope and a target to a country hungry for success after decades of slow progress often undercut by new problems. India 2020 became pretty much a peg for innumerable discussions, speeches and programmes.

Focused on a tight deadline and getting the book to press, with an above average but still modest print run of 4,000 hardback copies, there was not much time for discussion of the launch or the chief guest. It was decided, on Dr Kalam's suggestion, to invite the defence minister, George Fernandes, one-time firebrand trade union leader, by all accounts a good minister, and a troubleshooter for the Vajpayee-led coalition government which had around two dozen partners. As some of them were always on the verge of leaving the alliance, Fernandes would be sent to placate them. As the event date drew closer, there was some kind of indication from Fernandes that he would come for the launch, but uncertainty remained. And on the day of the launch itself this turned out to be justified – there was no word from him, and after much effort some information was gleaned that he had left on one of his troubleshooting trips to placate one of the coalition partners on some issue or the other.

It was thus a muted book launch in one of the seminar rooms at the India International Centre (IIC), Delhi. There was a photographer who took a video of Dr Kalam and Y.S. Rajan walking towards the main IIC building and it might still be with him. Precious footage, if it exists. The impact of the book was another thing altogether. Few books change attitudes and mindsets in the same way as *India 2020*.

For the next two decades there was actually a hope that the targets set out in the book would be achieved, not only industrial and scientific but also the intangibles that make for progress – a cleaner environment, a better lifestyle and greater harmony among people. The book went on to be translated into all the major Indian languages – Hindi, Malayalam, Tamil, Telugu, Marathi, Assamese ... The English edition alone sold more than 5,00,000 copies over the next few years. Whether the targets set out in *India 2020* were achieved or not, or were perhaps unrealistically high in some respects, the book is a reminder of the transformational power of a clear aim and a positive attitude.

While *India 2020* was a resounding success, Dr Kalam, who was at the centre of coordination and decision-making in key departments like the Defence Research and Development Organisation (DRDO), moved from South Block to an office in the annexe to Vigyan Bhavan as principal scientific adviser to the

Government of India. Here we undertook a follow-up to *India 2020* for which he came up with a title that would go on to become a catchphrase, *Ignited Minds*. He had a large office at Vigyan Bhavan, where we occasionally met to draft an outline for the book. On the work front, however, although he was always brimming with ideas, things were not moving so well. He was reticent to a fault and never discussed anything pertaining to work, but now and then, indirectly, the frustration showed through.

It was October 2001 and I had gone to meet him after his helicopter mishap on 30 September. The helicopter lost power just as it was landing at Bokaro. There were no casualties, but he was bruised. His main concern was that his family in Rameswaram should not get unduly worried, especially his elder brother. He was shaken too, though it would not be the only time his helicopter had to make a tricky landing – there was an incident in heavy rain later when he was President.

We had been making good progress on *Ignited Minds*, and as I was leaving he came to the door to see me out. At the time he would usually be in a well-worn blue suit, and while youthful, the grey seemed to be suddenly expanding. I do not know how common this is elsewhere, but it is a trait common among even senior politicians in India, and an entrancing one, this making the effort to walk across a capacious office all the way to the door – a kind of a bookmark that democracy exists and our leaders are not too big to observe ordinary courtesies. As he stood with the door open, I had to pass by him and was perfectly placed for the sudden question he asked: 'If I am no longer in government tomorrow, would you still be interested in the book?'

It was mildly put but it was not a question that one could prevaricate over or give a half-hearted answer to. At the heart of a commissioning editor's success is the conviction he brings to a project, and the trust he establishes with an author. Writing is an arduous skill for the best of authors. Even seasoned writers – journalists, for example, used to turning out a thousand words regularly – run into all kinds of problems when it comes to writing a book: often they lose focus, delay and abandon a project after putting in much time and effort researching. We had been working on *Ignited Minds* from sometime in 1999, and it had been persistence and faith that had brought us this far. An answer that reflected doubt would close the project.

Commissioning editors report to the editor-in-chief or publisher. It is they who can take a final call on a project. Even one midway such as this one. It was unlikely the project would be abandoned but would the ambitions connected with it remain – a very large print run (for the time) was being considered. It was possible the plans would be made more modest. As too the hopes on sales orders and the title status as super lead ... It could be, but in that moment of considering everything I said to him, truthfully enough, 'It will make no difference.' It couldn't have been truer.

A short time later – a month or two, or some weeks – he quit his high-ranking post. Apparently his proposals to the prime minister were going nowhere. Coordination was a problem and many were getting lost in the bureaucratic maze. He had an offer to teach from Anna University in Chennai and he accepted it. For all practical purposes, Kalam, after a distinguished career that earned him the respect of all the prime ministers he worked with, and an unrivalled array of honours from a grateful country, now at the age of seventy, could lead a life away from the politics, backbiting and power play of Delhi.

Generally speaking, life gives you back just as much as you give to it. Apparently Kalam had given much, much more, and there was a very substantial credit in his account.

Ignited Minds was nearing completion but the parts that remained would prove to be the hardest to do. I needed to go to Chennai and get his approvals on the text. I had to convince my publisher that the trip was necessary. As we worked on the text, I got late for the flight back. The aircraft gates were closed by the time I reached the check-in counter. I returned to the guest house, and we continued to work on the text. A subsequent trip was a couple of weeks later, in June 2002, to make some final revisions. As I boarded the flight the news broke: Kalam was the NDA's (the National Democratic Alliance was the coalition of around two dozen parties led by Atal Bihari Vajpayee) candidate for President. Victory seemed all but certain.

There would be many examples of publishing projects, sometimes the unlikeliest of ones or extremely modest ones, that take on a life of their own and a dimension hard to imagine. There are books with large advances that go into bookshops and look like non-starters whose sales are transformed by a twist of fate, such as a major award. After which from a mere few thousand at the start they go on to sell hundreds of thousands, given that the content to begin with had intrinsic appeal too. Or projects that looked like sure-shot successes that end up in the warehouse, with not an order coming in from any distributor.

In the case of *Ignited Minds*, released a couple of weeks before Kalam was sworn in, the title itself became an inspirational phrase that is still in use. The book took off. The 20,000 copies in the initial print run were gone in a week or two. The book was translated into every official Indian language. And in reprints the cover of the English edition proudly declares 'More than one million copies sold'.

The expectations around the book turned out to be quite true. But with Kalam that was more often than not the case. You could believe in the unlikeliest of things coming true. In every way he was one of the most successful presidents ever. Often, his success rubbed off on others too. There was much doubt raised by political commentators about a non-political president being able to do a good job. His level of popularity, however, was off the charts, going far beyond that of other, 'political', incumbents. He took charge from day one, assisted later by his adviser Major General R. Swaminathan, bringing high technology into the functioning of his office with the cables of computers, servers and printers snaking across the floor. Dr Kalam himself had a large computer console at his desk in 'The Study', as the President's office is called.

All through his tenure he was particular about maintaining the highest standards of his office. There was one room, and a staffer, assigned to sort, reply and highlight for action the thousands of letters received from only one region, and there would have been others to tackle the deluge of letters from other regions. In analysis and in the dry language of commentators, some things, some of the intangibles that we are not very good at recording, tend to get omitted. Thus in the analyses that followed after he demitted office, while there was much on his functioning as President and on the political aspects and his popularity, there wasn't much on the sheer sense of possibility that he brought to millions of Indians. There was a feel-good factor while he was there, more so while Atal Bihari Vajpayee was prime minister until 2004, but persisting later in Manmohan Singh's time too, although relations were cool with the Congress.

If his schedule was busy as President, it was no less so after he left office. Apart from the travel, intensive enough to faze people much younger, flying if distant, by car where flights not available or within a shorter distance, was the stream of visitors, a list of whom would be put up in his day's appointments. Aside from the visitors in Delhi was his phenomenal popularity across the country. Once on a visit to the World Book Fair at Delhi's Pragati Maidan, the scramble to meet him was so great the publisher's stand he was in was almost wrecked as bookshelves toppled in the surge of the crowd. His appearance at the Jaipur Literature Festival in 2015 was no less a draw than that of a rock star. The front lawn at the Diggi Palace was bursting at the seams. Not only that, the entryway, fairly wide, to the festival was equally packed with more people who wanted to listen to him.

Alongside the lectures, talks and speeches, as too launches and inaugurations (for book launches, he was the first choice of political leaders of all hues) for which he was much in demand from dozens of institutions and organizations, was his burgeoning writing career. For some of these, in pursuit of getting across an idea, he became motivated enough to do some research on his own. It is unusual for a President, incumbent or former, to reach out in the fashion that he did for his project *A Manifesto for Change*. He sent out questionnaires to elected representatives from grassroots level to Parliament to obtain practical inputs on improving governance, besides speaking with them. In addition he had been working on a series of development plans or vision documents for each state. He had managed to prepare these for most states. In the case of Uttar Pradesh, with whose chief minister at the time he enjoyed a good rapport, he prepared a development plan more than once. This included strengths, key industries, major employment avenues and ways to generate employment, which were dealt with in detail in the presentation. To the end, he was focused on making a difference. As retirements go, this was quite an ambitious one!

It was not possible to include in the book the surveys that featured in his presentations to the respective chief ministers, but they point to a very full schedule that he followed. A key element in it was the Ambassador car that took him to various destinations, in and around Delhi. It was presumably bulletproof but clunky and grimy. He was unassuming to a fault and a stickler for rules. Even if this meant that without adequate push to the concerned department maintenance of his residence could be slow. A bathroom upstairs adjacent to his office went slowly from bad to worse. Predictably, one day the sink itself collapsed. Once there was a power breakdown in a major storm and it became very dark in the afternoon. All there was as backup on that occasion was a single emergency light with which he sat in a room, while the rest of the house was in darkness until the lights came back on after quite some time.

As R.K. Prasad details in this account of working with him, more important was his stubbornness when it came to his health. There had been problems earlier too with it but his pace had become relentless as he tried to meet commitments. A previous, hectic visit before that last trip to Shillong had left him exhausted. He had become slow when he climbed the stairs to the first floor where he had his 'Ideas Lab' and his living quarters. All the signals pointed towards taking a pause. One wishes he had given himself more of a chance.

Krishan Chopra
August 2022
New Delhi

How This Book Came to Be

Sometime in 2014 I was on a flight with Dr A.P.J. Abdul Kalam from Thiruvananthapuram to Mumbai. We were seated in the front row. We had barely settled down in our seats after boarding when the third passenger in our row recognized Kalam and, having seen me talking to Kalam, asked me whether I was associated with him. I replied that I worked as his personal secretary. The passenger, Pratap Nair, was very excited. He said he wanted to be introduced to Kalam.

People asking to meet Kalam was nothing new to me. After his retirement, Kalam spent a great deal of his time travelling the length and breadth of the country giving talks, inaugurating projects and the like. He travelled mostly in economy class, and this was a matter of great pride (as well as a bit of a nuisance) for the airlines he flew. As soon as he was spotted, people would mob him, asking for autographs or photographs with them as they passed his seat. Some of them would place their small children and even infants on his lap for his blessings or for a picture, without so much as asking. The aisle would get blocked. To prevent this chaos, we always booked a front row seat for him and boarded last, usually to applause from the passengers.

Even though I was used to such requests, Pratap Nair was particularly persistent. He was from Kerala, and had his own business in Mumbai. It turned out he was a great fan of Kalam's. He was persuasive enough to follow up with me and later met Kalam with his family, though only once. He also went on to publish a collection of Kalam's speeches in 2016.

I had forgotten all about him, but shortly after Kalam passed away in 2015, Nair got in touch with me again. 'You have spent so many years with Kalam, you must write about him,' he told me. Such a thought had never crossed my mind though Kalam himself had encouraged me to write a book and said he would write the foreword for it. However, I was hardly a writer, so Kalam's request was received in one ear and let out through the other. But Nair was persistent, as persistent as he had been when he was following up with me on his request to meet Kalam. He told me he would find me a writer. I would simply have to go to Mumbai and talk to the writer and he would write my account of Kalam for me. I said I would think about it, but I suspect he knew he would have to take matters into his own hands. He then told me he would send the writer to Delhi, and I finally agreed.

So it was that in 2018 K.P. Sivakumar, the freelance writer chosen by Pratap Nair, came to Delhi. The first draft of this book was the result of several days of conversation with Sivakumar, reliving my memories of Abdul Kalam, whom I had served for about twenty years. During those years I had probably spent more time with him than with any other person from my family.

For the first several years that I worked with him there was never any conversation between us that touched on the personal. And even afterwards, though he would touch upon some personal matters, he was mostly reticent. He especially did not like to discuss anything related to his health or any negative (or for that matter positive) events in his life. Kalam never went over matters, negative or positive, nor mulled over any developments – at least not with us assistants who handled all his work till the end of his life. I think it was just the way Kalam was: he refused to dwell on anything from the past and preferred to remain engrossed in doing what was required in the present and to look ahead at what to do next. I never heard him comment on anything from the past.

Whatever it was, he eventually became one among my circle of first concerns in life, and his death was like the loss of a close family member. In this book, I have attempted to put together some of my experiences while working for him from 1993 to 2015. It describes some of his personal traits unknown to those outside his intimate circle and also some of which he omitted mentioning in his memoirs due to reasons best known to him.

1

A New Job

I cannot think of anything I can say about my life until I began working for A.P.J. Abdul Kalam. There seemed nothing distinctive about it, and there seemed nothing distinctive about my surroundings and the people in it either.

In 1985 I arrived in Delhi from Palakkad in Kerala, having been selected for a job in the central government after passing the Staff Services Selection Commission exams. I was quite blank – in every sense of the word – when I arrived. I knew little about anything, having lived all my life in small towns (in the pre-Internet age). My father had been a state government officer in Kerala, and I had studied in a government school and graduated from Calicut University. On being selected for the job, I was asked to report at the defence ministry in Delhi. My father accompanied me to Delhi, dropped me at a friend's home and returned immediately.

I was appointed as a junior secretarial assistant in the defence ministry. I was there for a little over five years. In

1991–1992 I was posted to the defence minister's office. This was something I had wanted. In fact, I had got in touch with many people requesting for this posting. Most of them could not understand what the attraction of this posting was as it did not entail a change in my designation or level. But for me, a job in a minister's office meant that I would be allotted a house quicker.

I never got to meet the defence minister, of course. There was a strict hierarchy in the office, as there is in most government offices, and layers of bureaucracy. Only the political secretary and the minister's inner circle of friends and advisers got to meet him. Anyway, most ministers are more comfortable with their close staff speaking their own language. To my delight I was allotted my quarters within a short time, but the work was killing. Whereas earlier I would finish work by 7 or 7.30 p.m., I discovered that in a minister's office work never ends. It used to be at least 9.30 p.m. before I was released for the day, and there was no guarantee of a free Saturday or Sunday either. I had pushed hard to get there, and found myself in a fine mess.

I worked in the defence minister's office in South Block from 1991 to 1993, till the minister resigned after the Mumbai bomb blasts in March to take over as chief minister of Maharashtra. The office then got disbanded and the staff were posted out. I now returned to my previous office, which was the office of the scientific adviser to the defence minister. Little did I know that, workwise, it would be out of the frying pan and into the fire for me.

Kalam had been appointed a year earlier, in 1992, as scientific adviser to the minister of defence and was also chief of the Department of Defence Research and Development (popularly known as DRDO, the Defence Research and Development Organisation). I had seen him earlier, perhaps first in 1989 in South Block, when he was visiting from Hyderabad. I had heard about the space programme and knew he was the person behind India's missile programmes. He was then director of the Missile Laboratory, based in Hyderabad, and director of the missile programme. He kept a busy schedule and spoke English with a very strong Tamil accent. I knew little else beyond that.

I did not get to interact with Kalam the first three or four months after my posting back in the same old office. This is because seniority plays a big role in what is assigned to you and determines access to the top man. Those above me in the office were of the level of senior private secretary and staff officer to Kalam and all had 15–20 years of experience in the same office handling confidential matters. They were also experts in crisis management.

In such highly sensitive offices handling secret work, no junior or new person is allowed access to certain documents, papers and information. Some categories of work come to them only after a few months of service and background verification by security agencies. Their entry to and exit from office is always monitored.

Then one day, I got to interact with Kalam. An important fax landed on my table. The seniors were not around. The fax was for the department, so I went into Kalam's room and gave it to him. He asked me my name and where I was from. He spoke to me for ten minutes. He was dressed in a bush shirt and trousers, his favoured clothes even as President later. He seemed not at all interested in his appearance. For formal events he would wear a suit.

The next day onward he began to send work directly to me. 'Call that guy,' or 'Call that man,' he would say, referring to me. He drowned me with work. There were fifty-eight laboratories across the country under him, and one of my responsibilities was to coordinate with different labs and organize his travel to each place. He gave me so much work that I was overwhelmed and thoroughly confused. I even began passing on some of the work to my seniors. Kalam came out of his room one day and saw that others were doing the work he had handed me. Later, I figured that he was testing me. To get adjusted to his way and pace of working took me some time. It was a tough situation.

H. Sheridon and I, Kalam's two personal assistants, occupied the same room. It was a kind of anteroom where people sat while they waited to meet Kalam. Kalam's own room was a large hall with a sizeable conference area; a seating area with sofas, where he conducted large committee meetings on all Mondays and met his important guests; and of course his desk and workspace. I was forever marching up and down from my room to his. I had truly landed in the fire. I had had enough at the minister's office working till 9.30 p.m., but here work could carry on till 11 p.m. and occasionally later.

Kalam's reliance on me grew. Whenever he needed some assistance after office hours, he would summon Sheridon and me. I responded unhesitatingly, though I disliked the long and late work hours. Whether the work was assigned after 7 p.m. or after midnight, I did it. I never refused to oblige him on holidays either. Yes, the long hours in the minister's office had bothered me. But I quickly gathered that Kalam was not an ordinary official who worked to please others for personal gain, but one determined to achieve something for the country's pride, peace and prosperity. I set aside my personal chores and attended to his needs even long after regular office hours.

But work under Kalam frequently took on horrific proportions. A call would come at around 9 p.m. and it would take me close to an hour to reach Kalam's office, crawling through Delhi's almost unmoving traffic. After preparations and preliminary discussions, the real work would begin at around 11.30 p.m. The work would go on till after midnight, till the first draft of the necessary document had been completed. Then Kalam would go over it, scrutinizing it minutely for its coherence and order of paragraphs, annotations and structure of sentences. He would come up with a list of major and minor corrections. It would be close to three in the morning when I reached home after incorporating the changes he wanted and finalizing the document.

Sometimes he would draw a blank on ideas but would still dictate something or give me some talking points. It then fell on me to create a document from those scraps. I would have to collect the background information and make a six- or seven-page report, sometimes by 1 a.m. But the next morning I had to report to work at nine, as usual. If it was later than 10 p.m. he would send a vehicle to take me to his place. He lived in a DRDO guest house all those years. It had one bedroom, a bathroom and a dining room. And the dining room was where he would meet his guests. Everywhere he lived he confined himself to one room. That was all the space he would occupy. There would be books and papers crammed into every available space. Even at Rashtrapati Bhavan, he occupied only a tiny area.

My regular work too was as hectic as ever. The regular staff, including me, would be in the office by 9 a.m. But Kalam would start calling us on the office phone from 8.45 a.m., to issue instructions for the day and to confirm the day's schedule, and, if required, to shuffle around meetings that were relatively unimportant or could be postponed. Soon we too started to reach the office at 8.45 a.m., to scribble down his dictation on the phone. He would arrive in office at around 10.30 a.m. With him in the cabin, work would flow at a terrific pace. The phones would ring continuously, with calls from various DRDO establishment heads wanting to speak to the chief.

One barely got the time to drink a glass of water. There was non-stop work often till 6.30–7 p.m. There were many days when we sat down to lunch at 4 p.m. At lunchtime he would often come over to our room and hand us the work directly. 'Postpone your lunch and finish this work first,' he would say. We staff would do his bidding, having lunch only after handing over the work so we could eat in peace. He would have his regular two chapattis and curry brought in from the department canteen. He was as uninterested in food as he was in clothes.

Only in 1996 did I get an official telephone for my residence. Before that, if Kalam wanted me over after office hours, he would send his car to pick me up from my home. The driver would alert me and take me to Kalam's office. Kalam got the phone sanctioned for me. After that, he began to call whenever he wanted work done. He would usually call at 10.30 p.m. He would begin by saying, 'Hello, you, note down ...' or 'You guy, note down ...' There were no preliminary niceties or greetings on his part. I had to identify the caller from his voice, which was by then all too familiar to me, of course. Often he wanted me to connect with the heads of the DRDO labs and give them a slot to call Kalam. On such days he would conclude the call saying, 'Don't sleep till everyone calls me back.' I would remain awake until it was confirmed to me that all the heads of institutions with whom Kalam wished to speak had reverted to him.

Thus, sitting in his guest house fifteen kilometres away, Kalam used to keep me working late into the night. Sometimes my son would answer the phone and call out to me, 'He [Kalam] is calling.' Kalam would then begin to speak in Malayalam to my son. My wife was working as a teacher in a school. While we were at work on weekdays, our son was sent to a crèche. On Saturdays we used to leave him with a neighbour. But one Saturday my neighbour wasn't at home and I had some urgent work at the office. I had no choice but to take my son along. I had to ask for special permission from security to get him in. I made him sit in a chair behind me. At 11 a.m., when Kalam reached the office and found the small boy sitting behind me, he asked who it was. I told him it was my son and his name was Ajay, and he said, 'Oh, this is the guy who answers my calls.' He added, 'Oh, don't take him around like this. Put him in school.' I told him Ajay was not yet four and to join a school he had to be five. After a brief silence, Kalam went into his room. He did not seem happy that a child had been brought to the office. After about two hours, he summoned me and asked me to go home. Kalam was concerned about my son's lunch. That was why he allowed me to return home in the middle of the day.

Around that time, there was a burglary in our neighbourhood. This naturally sent a wave of fear through our home. My wife insisted that I be home before 9 p.m. daily. I had to convey this to Kalam. He listened keenly and went away without comment. But after that day he never called me for late-night work. I would complete my day's assignments between 9.30 and 10.30 p.m. and leave the office, after which he didn't call me. I realized that when he was making us work as much as he did it was not out of insensitivity to his juniors but because he was so deeply immersed in his work that he forgot everything else. Once he was alert to any real difficulty in our lives he was quick to react and was sensitive in his response.

From 1995 to December 1999 (when he left the post), he would often drop me at my place on his way home. It was hardly on his way though. I lived in a place called Gole Market, which is close to Connaught Place, and his guest house was in Asiad Village, some fifteen kilometres away. There was a shorter route that he could have taken if he did not have to drop me. But he never bothered about these things. It startled my neighbourhood quite a bit in the beginning, my being dropped back in a car with a beacon light accompanied by police pilot and escort.

On a number of occasions our office worked like a control room during important national defence missions. Sheridon and I had to be extra alert then. Sheridon was at the same level as me at work, but had joined a couple of years earlier. We shared the work more or less equally, and when one of us had to be away, the entire load had to be borne by the other since Kalam never allowed anyone else to take charge.

Kalam was away most weekends leading some strategic mission or visiting distant labs to check on the progress of various projects. The Saturdays and Sundays he was away from Delhi were working days for the labs. In his absence we remained the sole contact point, attending to innumerable inquiries. Most of the time Kalam would be in Balasore in Orissa, his mission range area. Or he would be in Hyderabad or Bangalore, where some major projects were under way. He would instruct one of us to be available in the office by his phone on Saturdays and holidays till a specific time in the afternoon. There were no mobile phones in those days, and that was the only way to communicate important information to him.

Kalam too would call us frequently, passing on critical information from wherever he was, which we had to relay to the higher authorities in Delhi. As details of his location were kept confidential, only we were privy to where he was. We, of course, could not divulge his whereabouts to anyone. He used to remind us on the phone not to tell anybody where he was. Then he would ask, 'OK. What will you say if someone asks where I am?' We had to supply a wrong answer about his location to satisfy him. For example, if he was in Orissa, we had to say he was in Kerala; if he was in Pokhran, we would say he was visiting Orissa. Our inventiveness in giving callers misleading answers about his real location always made him satisfied and happy. Such tactics kept his movements and information about his plans secret, known only to a select few. Kalam had us well convinced that ours was an extremely sensitive office.

Even the mounting work pressure couldn't snatch away the satisfaction we derived from our work, for we knew that whatever we did for Kalam was for the sake of the nation. Knowing that you are involved in something critical to the country had an uplifting effect. And directly reporting to Kalam had its own gratification.

However, I must admit that the office pressure sometimes got too much for me. From 1994 to 1996, and occasionally after that up to 1998, from time to time I tried every method to get a transfer out of Kalam's office. I tried very, very hard, but somehow could not manage it. I even told Kalam to help me get a transfer to the Indian Space Research Organisation (ISRO) in Thiruvananthapuram, but he ignored my requests. In 1997 Kalam was conferred the Bharat Ratna, India's highest civilian award, for his contribution to India's defence technology, and people started to recognize his office too. That gave me a shot of enthusiasm to continue with him. People began to treat us with greater regard in South Block, since we were working with the only Bharat Ratna awardee in government. And in 1998 came preparations for the Pokhran-II tests. During that period there was no way we could move anywhere. We were his eyes and ears, and we knew too much.

After Pokhran-II, Kalam mellowed down a lot and work too settled into a saner routine. He would leave office at a decent hour and rarely asked us to be at the office on Saturdays or holidays. He was well past his retirement age, which was fifty-eight at the time. It was extended to sixty in May 1998 by the then government. But Kalam was sixty-seven in 1998 and was principal scientific adviser to the Government of India, a post specifically created for him after his Bharat Ratna. He was certainly tripping up progress for others down the line. The government had approved his continuance at the post as a special case till further orders. Slowly, the others down the pecking order at the DRDO began to murmur.

2

Shifting Sands

Kalam spent seven long years at the DRDO. As a key resource person in various high-profile missions like the missile programme, and as head of the DRDO later, Kalam had to work closely with several prime ministers and defence ministers he served. P.V. Narasimha Rao, H.D. Deve Gowda and I.K. Gujral are among the prime ministers he worked with, and Sharad Pawar, Pramod Mahajan, Mulayam Singh Yadav and George Fernandes the defence ministers. When Pramod Mahajan was appointed defence minister, he said he was fortunate to work with people like Kalam in the ministry. It was unheard of for a cabinet minister to acknowledge his scientific adviser in such a manner. All the prime ministers and defence ministers appeared to genuinely respect Kalam for the credibility and honesty with which he carried out his role as scientific adviser to the defence minister and chief of the DRDO.

In 1998, when A.B. Vajpayee was prime minister, the country hurriedly prepared for the second Pokhran test.

At the helm was Kalam. He was travelling frequently to the mission area and the objective of his activities was not disclosed even to us. He would ask us to get approval for an Avro aircraft and helicopter from the Air Force at a specific time and date to visit a specific place. We would do that. As to what happened at these places during his visit, I had simply no clue. Eventually the test blasts took place on 11 May and again on 13 May 1998. Thereafter, compliments and criticism rained on Kalam, who remained unaffected by both.

By the end of 1999, the discontent brewing against Kalam was quite palpable in the corridors of South Block and among the seniormost scientists. His long and continuing tenure as both chief of the DRDO and principal scientific adviser to the Government of India had begun to rankle the senior echelon at the DRDO, as they felt their prospects were being obstructed by this man.

The complaining murmurs – that he had been in the top position for so long and was well past his retirement age – began to get louder and louder. Pressure was mounting on the government to move out Kalam and to clear the way for his successors. But Kalam was hale and hearty and the government did not have sufficient reason to move him from his post.

As someone who was among his personal staff, I would get to hear a little of the tittle-tattle going on in the corridors of South Block: Kalam was too old, he was better at management than science, etc. The clique that wanted him out must have felt they had reached the end of the road as far as their career progress was concerned.

The disaffection didn't stop with talk behind Kalam's back. He too was watchful and wary, I noticed. He too must have heard about the murmurs from his sources of information, or maybe he sensed the mood. Not that we knew, as he never discussed anything with us. In a position such as his, one is all alone, one does not know who is working against them. The top man must be scared of his own shadow. But the government was with him, and the others had no voice. In fact, Kalam was so high profile that nobody even knew who the number two in the organization was.

One evening, an officer from a closed circle told me about the imminent shifting of Kalam. I promptly told Kalam about it. I said, 'Sir, there is some talk going on, there is a rumour that your successor has been selected and orders are soon to be issued.'

Kalam was surprised. 'Oh! Is that so? I am not aware of that. Who is going to be my successor?' he asked me. I replied that I did not know, and suggested that he had better check with the defence minister, George Fernandes. He instantly asked me to connect him to Fernandes through the secure phone in his room. Soon the minister was on the phone. Kalam signalled that I remain beside him, as he used to do when he wanted us to take notes of his conversation.

As I stood there, I could hear the minister speak. After a brief exchange of formal greetings, Kalam asked, 'Sir, what happened? Have you finalized the selection of my successor from that list?'

Kalam had provided the minister with a shortlist of candidates of his choice for consideration for his post. In 1999, with the pressure of the Pokhran tests behind him, he was a bit more free and friendly, and had been working on identifying a person to take on his role. He had made a list of his preferred candidates and sent it to the higher-ups.

Fernandes replied, 'No, Kalam. How can I select someone without informing you? Nothing has happened. Don't worry. I will keep you informed.'

Ten minutes after this conversation there was a knock on the door and four people led by a senior scientist with a paper in his hand entered. The senior scientist told Kalam, 'Sir, I have been appointed scientific adviser to the defence minister. Here is the order. I have to take charge tomorrow.' Kalam expressed absolutely no emotion outwardly. He simply congratulated the scientist and his team and sat with them to discuss some aspects of the work the role entailed.

The visitors left, and still Kalam did not say anything. He swiftly wound up the day's work and prepared to leave. He expressed no surprise as to why George Fernandes, a close friend, or at least a regular associate of his for some time now, had not told him the truth about finalizing his successor. I detected a slight flush on his face. It would not have been noticeable to any other bystander.

We hurriedly closed the office in an hour and left. I knew he would not vent his ire at what happened – not that day, nor the next day, nor ever. He never dwelt on adverse events (or even positive events, as I have said earlier), never expressed hatred or desire for vengeance. That was Kalam, every single time.

The appointee had been the second on Kalam's shortlist. Generally, other than the first name, all other names on any shortlist are only for formality's sake. It was a clear snub to Kalam. I knew that he was taken aback by Fernandes's unseating of him in this manner and by the minister's disregard for his suggestions for his replacement. Not only from the flush on his face that I believed only I could detect but also because he didn't call me later that night. Usually, after I left office at 8–8.30 p.m. there would be a call from him between 10 and 11 p.m. There was no call that day.

So far, Kalam's word had been the final word in all matters concerning the department. He had never been overruled by the minister. Fernandes and he shared a special bond. Both lived alone. Fernandes would bring his car up to our office gate to pick up Kalam for a dinner out, usually of appam and stew, which was Kalam's favourite. Fernandes, who was from Mangalore, loved this kind of food. They would usually go to Sagar Ratna, a restaurant that served Mangalorean food, or to the India International Centre. They would walk in casually, and the moment the staff there saw them they would reserve a table for them in a corner, distant from everybody else.

The next day, Kalam came to office at the usual time to hand over charge to the new incumbent. And he simply stood there without a room to sit and work in. However, we managed to convert an adjoining small room which was occupied by his technical staff officer into an office for him.

Kalam was elevated to the post of principal scientific adviser to the Government of India in 1997 after the Bharat Ratna was conferred on him. Perhaps the government would not have wanted the media to report that India's missile man was shunted out the way he was. In moving him out they had elevated him and created an office for him. By early January 2000, after spending about fifteen days working from a small room next to his old office, Kalam was granted a new, bigger office space in the Vigyan Bhavan Annexe, some two kilometres from South Block. It took several months for the staff and facilities to be put in place at the new office.

Before shifting out, Kalam asked me if I wished to go with him. I happily said yes. I was relieved that I would be stationed out of the DRDO head office. I was sure that the new head of the DRDO would not be entirely comfortable with me as I was known as 'Kalam's man'. I was certain that he would not assign any important work to me. He would fear I would pass on comments and comparisons on his functioning to Kalam. Kalam requested that I too should be sent to work with him, but his successor wrote back to Kalam saying he needed me for the smooth running of his office. He said my absence would handicap the functioning of his office. So, in the year 2000, I was separated from Kalam, while Sheridon followed Kalam to his new office, in a new grade.

The new chief was indeed not too happy with me. After all, I had worked with Kalam for so long and so closely that there was a trust deficit from the outset. Anything that I did might be thought of as coming from Kalam. The new chief thought I was not reliable. That he only assigned work to his man indirectly showed his dislike for me. He ignored my comments and suggestions. He had his man in office and it was my duty to train him in the various functions of the office. He also marked me with a low grade in my annual report.

In hindsight, I feel not everybody could work with Kalam. Even those who used to look upon us with a tinge of envy surely did not envy the work we had to do day and night, which is abnormal in a government set-up.

Without Kalam, the office resembled an empty festival ground. There was only routine work but it was not hectic and I was relieved. It was a more bureaucratic routine that I settled down to, a nine-to-six schedule. I did get a lot of time for myself.

I could never understand why a person like Kalam was the object of so much envy to certain people in his organization. He was neutral towards others and neither favoured nor disliked anyone. Till date I have not been able to come up with a satisfactory answer. He did not encourage those who were not relevant to his work to penetrate his orbit. He was not a party animal, but rather a party pooper. He never did anything that might blemish the decorum of his office. He would appear at parties only when they were organized by the department and unavoidable, and that too just as the party was about to wind down. He put in an appearance to mark his attendance. He politely declined most lunch and dinner invitations from the armed forces. As a result, Kalam was a person not accessible for any kind of entertainment.

However, he was a popular guide, philosopher and intellectual sounding board well appreciated by many scientists, bureaucrats, people's representatives, ministers and statesmen – excluding of course that bunch of people who wanted him out to pave a path ahead for themselves, who envied his direct access to the highest levels of government. After all, from 1994 onward, Kalam was placed in the Z+ security category, which distanced him from common gatherings too.

Kalam had direct access to the Prime Minister's Office (PMO). He only had to ask for an appointment and he would get one within half an hour. That could have irked many bureaucrats and some politicians too.

A person like Kalam can never remain idle for lack of work. He would always find projects, wherever he was. When his work increased at his new office, I began to receive calls from him to assist him after office hours. He would say, 'Come to my place this evening. I have work to do.' I was also summoned whenever Sheridon was on leave.

In November 2001, Kalam abruptly resigned from the post of principal scientific adviser to the Government of India, apparently after some differences with the minister for science and technology, who allegedly disliked Kalam's way of getting things done.

Immediately upon resigning, Kalam left for Chennai, where he had been offered the position of Professor of Technology and Societal Transformation at Anna University. It was a post specifically created for him. It had been his long-cherished dream to communicate with the youth of the country. So on assuming this role, he began to travel across the country, delivering lectures to students on topics of scientific import.

Kalam seldom spoke about anything personal with me. I don't know whether he opened his heart to anyone at all. Perhaps he did; he had friends from his ISRO days and a couple of others who were of his generation whom he was pretty close to. And he and I were quite distantly placed in the matter of age. People like to imagine that he was a solitary man and link many aspects of his personality to his being single and 'lonely'. But I never felt at any time that he was lonely. He was always either on the phone or reading books on science or philosophy.

Everything for him was about work. He took no holidays and was disinclined to allow us to take holidays. 'Festival? What festival?' he would ask, when we asked leave for a ceremony or festival. But he would unfailingly call me and Sheridon on Onam and Christmas to wish us. He himself never observed any festivals, never visited any place of worship. We would call to wish him on the two days of Eid. He would happily accept the greetings with a thank you and immediately give us some work to do. He told me once that he used to pray five times daily, and we knew he used to pray in his room, but I never saw him offering prayers. Later, when he became President, I noticed that there was always a prayer book and a rosary sticking out of his pocket. But in his official avatar and in public view there was no hint whatsoever of any religious observances on his part. He was deeply private and observed the dignity and religious neutrality of his office with great ease.

3

'Something Is Cooking'

Kalam's academic days in Chennai were going splendidly, from what I heard. It must have been a relief for him from the sniping that continued to come his way even in his position as principal scientific adviser to the Government of India.

As principal scientific adviser too, Kalam could have been laid-back about his work, but he was the kind of person who managed to create work even if there was no pressure on him to do any. Sheridon had gone with him to his new office, but, as mentioned earlier, I too was summoned outside of office hours or on holidays when Kalam was particularly loaded with work or Sheridon was away. Perhaps that was because he found it easier to assign work to me rather than to start from scratch with a new person.

Kalam would reach out to the heads of institutions, such as the Indian Institute of Science, and universities and generate reports on various topics which he would pass on to the science and technology minister. And

Kalam continued to present reports to everybody concerned, even if no concrete steps were initiated on his reports.

Kalam managed to paint himself into the same corner with the science and technology minister as he had with the defence minister. He could visit the prime minister directly, and was never asked to approach him through the minister. So there was a kind of cold war between Kalam and the minister. Once Kalam was made to wait for several hours for an audience with the minister. Normally a person at his level would not be kept waiting for more than ten minutes. This happened more than once. Kalam must have realized he was an unwanted man and was deliberately being put down.

He had his well-wishers and contacts, and one of them was Professor A. Kalanidhi, then vice chancellor of Anna University in Chennai. Kalanidhi offered Kalam the post of Professor Emeritus and Professor of Technology and Societal Transformation, a new department created at the university. Of course, Kalanidhi had to get permission from the government to use his discretionary power for this hire, but Kalanidhi was well known and politically well connected. In no time at all, everything was organized for Kalam. And, one fine morning, Kalam announced he was quitting.

I too attended the farewell party organized by the Department of Science and Technology for Kalam.

Senior scientists and the minister were present. Nobody asked Kalam why he had quit. The next morning he left, carrying one suitcase with two or three trousers and shirts and some books. The DRDO informally permitted him to continue to occupy the flat he had been holding for a long time. Most of his belongings remained in the DRDO guest house until 2003.

In Chennai, Kalam was treated like royalty. He had a separate department, guest quarters, a small office and two or three administrative staff to assist him. Food was delivered to him from the university canteen or was prepared by his attendants. Kalanidhi was happy. He had a Bharat Ratna as faculty. And Kalam hit the ground running, as usual, getting down to work the very next day of his arrival in Chennai.

Kalam gave lectures at the university. I have heard various opinions on his lectures. Some enjoyed them, some said they were too technical and some even said they were too simplistic for the MTech level. He also continued to travel across the country as invitations came pouring in from colleges, universities and NGOs. He had contracted an assistant to help him with his speeches and presentations. This assistant followed him to Delhi when he became President and worked in Rashtrapati Bhavan for about ten months. He was a university-trained man, not particularly aware of protocol of bureaucratic hierarchy. He was informal with the President even during visits from heads of nations. This irritated the Rashtrapati Bhavan bureaucracy, which found a way to remove him.

Kalam was quite good at managing the media, in a way no one even in politics managed. Something or the other kept appearing about him in the newspapers. He did not actually reveal anything, but he would say something that would get published.

Kalam's Anna University stint was indeed a splendid one for him. During this time, he was given several awards, notable among them being an award from the Maharaja of Jodhpur for his contributions to the nation and for inspiring the youth. Occasionally he would visit Delhi and stay in the DRDO guest house rooms that had been allocated to him. The rooms were always available to him in honour of his Bharat Ratna and his contributions to the national defence programme.

The National Democratic Alliance (NDA) led by the Bharatiya Janata Party (BJP) was looking for a presidential candidate. The names doing the rounds in the capital's corridors those days were of the then President, K.R. Narayanan; the then Vice President, Krishan Kant; and the governor of Maharashtra, P.C. Alexander. The NDA was under pressure to find a candidate acceptable across the political spectrum as the BJP was in bad shape. The Godhra incident, which led to riots in Gujarat, was fresh in people's minds. The NDA wanted a pro-Muslim face. N. Chandrababu Naidu suggested Kalam as a potential candidate to Prime Minister Vajpayee. He appealed to everyone across the country, from the very young to the old. One day Sheridon received a call from the PMO asking for Kalam's telephone number. We later learnt that Vajpayee then called up Kalam at around midnight on his landline and asked him if he would be willing to be a presidential candidate if his name was proposed. We also learnt that Kalam told him something like this, which was so typical of him: 'No problem, I'm ready. I have no political background, no support. But you are with me, and I am ready.'

The next day Kalam talked about this indirectly to Sheridon, but did not tell him everything. 'See, I have to go to Delhi. Something is cooking.' Those were his words. And his typical 'You be ready.' At that time I was on a long train journey from Delhi to Palakkad, and I saw a small news report on the possibility of Kalam being the NDA's choice for President. Given the nature of my office, I had been provided with a mobile phone, a rarity then in government departments. In those days it cost sixteen rupees a minute to make a call. Receiving a call cost the same. I called Sheridon. Was the news correct? Yes, you be ready, he told me, as if echoing Kalam. I told him to put my name along with his for the new office. Not everyone gets to work for the President of the nation.

There was a buzz among the passengers in the train who had also read the report. I did not tell the family anything. In any case the trip was jinxed. My wife's handbag, which I had hung from a hook above her berth in the second AC compartment, was stolen. My new cell phone, some money and our tickets had been in the bag.

We got down at Vijayawada station and filed a complaint with the railway police, but they were callous and unhelpful. At Palakkad, our final destination, I filed another FIR. We had lost belongings worth ten thousand rupees, quite a sum for a middle-class family even in 2002. We had lost our house keys too, so we had to call a neighbour in Delhi and ask them to have the lock changed. Given all this, I returned in fifteen days' time, in early June, cancelling my long leave.

Kalam's name came as a thorough surprise and the Congress and parties aligned with it had no substantial reason to oppose it; nor could they find an equally remarkable choice. So they supported him. The left parties and the Forward Bloc chose former INA revolutionary Captain Lakshmi Sehgal as their candidate to oppose Kalam.

When Kalam submitted his nomination, he was flanked by top leaders of both the ruling and the opposition parties. This was a historic event indeed, all of them standing shoulder to shoulder to support a single presidential candidate. Kalam came to Parliament House in a procession consisting of Prime Minister Atal Bihari Vajpayee, Home Minister L.K. Advani, External Affairs Minister Jaswant Singh, Defence Minister George Fernandes, three chief ministers of the time – Naveen Patnaik, Chandrababu Naidu and Mayawati – Trinamool Congress leader Mamata Banerjee, and leaders of the Samajwadi Party, Mulayam Singh and Amar Singh. I still remember that scene. The first set of papers was filed by the NDA leaders. The Congress filed the second set of nomination papers that contained sixty proposers and sixty seconders with Sonia Gandhi in the lead.

Once the nominations were filed, Kalam resumed his stay at the DRDO guest house. The DRDO was only too happy to have him; it was a matter of pride that a former head of the institution was going to be President. He had to do a lot of correspondence, contacting members of Parliament (MPs) for their vote, especially party leaders, and so on. There was a tremendous amount of work taking place in his rooms. Sheridon was with him. I was working at the DRDO headquarters. Soon Kalam called me. 'You also come, start working from my office.' I was on cloud nine, but reality hit me not long afterwards. My boss would not let me go. 'Sir, I would love to work for you. Please do talk to my boss, or he won't relieve me,' I told Kalam.

He agreed to do that. The next day he called my boss and informed him that he needed me and that I should be relieved. My boss could not say no to the President-designate. Turning to me, he said, 'Your boss is calling you. You can go and work with him from tomorrow.'

On seeing me at the guest house office, Kalam said, without any preliminaries, niceties or greetings, 'See, now we have a lot of work to accomplish. We have to send letters to all the 740-odd MPs and ministers. I have to visit select states and meet people for their support.' Election day was a week later. Kalam won with an overwhelming majority, garnering 922,884 electoral votes, while his opponent could only manage 107,366.

There was a flood of phone calls and visits from people to wish him. I had to handle all that too, and also arrange travel and stay for his relatives visiting from Rameswaram to attend the swearing-in ceremony. My 'deputation' to Kalam's office was only temporary. That gesture from my boss did not mean I could permanently work with Kalam. And Kalam was giving me what looked like full-time work. I expressed my apprehensions to him. 'No. You don't have to bother. The President wants you. Just come here and start working,' he told me.

A week later, I went to my previous office to collect some of my belongings. Naturally, my boss there was not at all pleased to see me. He commented on how I had begun to work in another office without a formal posting order. An order was eventually issued specifying my new assignment and I was attached to the President's office.

From the second week of July 2002, I assumed the role of private secretary to the President-designate, first working from the DRDO guest house and towards the end of July from Rashtrapati Bhavan. There is a notion that only All India Service (AIS) officers possess the capability to work in such offices – that myth was given a go-by and Sheridon and I were appointed. And we managed the work of the highest office with dignity and kept its stature intact, thereby bringing no ill repute to the President himself. After our departure in 2007, the new regime reversed the practice and made it mandatory to appoint only AIS officers to that office. Clearly, some still entertained the misconception that only AIS officers had the potential to work in these posts.

After Kalam won, he had to prepare a list of invitees for the swearing-in ceremony. Apart from his family – his brother, his niece and his brother's grandchildren, and a few others – his invitees were academics and doctors and so on. There were no politicians on his list.

That was unique. Normally the swearing-in is attended by sitting MPs and eminent persons from Delhi (not India, note). Kalam also wanted ten students each from ten different government schools in Delhi to attend as a rare gesture to the youth, who till then were largely ignored by everyone. That was a new thing. The Parliament staff were upset. How would they manage so many students?

The home ministry could not protest or block the inclusion of students for very long. It was the President-designate asking for them, and they had to honour his demands. They arranged for the selected students to be brought in for the ceremony and then taken back. I must say it was all done beautifully; after all, so many checks needed to be done, especially since Parliament had been attacked only a year ago, in 2001. Nobody even thought that such a thing as bringing in students to Parliament could happen. Sheridon and I did not put our names on the invitee list, but Kalam insisted that our names and our wives' names were on the list.

Now fell on the organizers the task of persuading the President to get out of his standard shirt, pants and jacket and into a bandgala suit. 'I will not wear it,' he said. 'I'll wear my own regular clothes.' Officials tried to gently persuade him to wear the bandgala: 'This is the dress for the ceremony, sir.' Of course, if he had stuck to his no, he would have had his way, being the President, but he relented.

A clothesmaker arrived in his room soon afterwards and suggested a new style for him, pointing out that he did not even have a proper jacket. Surprisingly, he agreed. Someone also proposed that his hair be cut short, and a newspaper even did a story on how he would look without his signature hairstyle. He had agreed to a bandgala but firmly put his foot down in the matter of his hair. What I am should be acceptable, take me as I am, otherwise drop me, that was his attitude. However, his hair was trimmed neatly for the day.

Unsurprisingly, Kalam spent hours preparing his speech, and there were twenty-four drafts in all. He wanted an impactful one – verses from Kabir and the *Thirukkural* were added. The verse in Hindi, which had to be transliterated for him in English, fetched a lot of applause. I left the President-designate's office at 1 a.m. on 24 July. The swearing-in was the next day.

After the ceremony Kalam was taken from Parliament House to the President's office in a car bearing the national emblem instead of a number plate. The car was accompanied by angarakshaks, military personnel, and a horse carriage brought out only for swearing-in ceremonies and on Republic Day. Nobody could accompany him. No one could be in the car with him. I had to follow in another car allowed inside Rashtrapati Bhavan.

Kalam pointed to Sheridon and me and said the two of us needed to be accommodated. Sheridon and I got an office each. 'If there is no work order for them to work here, they will stop coming. Issue orders for these two,' said Kalam to the officials in charge. Thus we were given formal orders deputing us from the Ministry of Defence to the President's office. As all orders go, ours began with 'You are hereby asked to report ... etc.' For us the reporting was literal and immediate. At 3 p.m. on 25 July, the day of the swearing-in, we began work at Rashtrapati Bhavan. And so did the President.

Again, this was not a President who would treat his job as a sinecure. It was his nature to create work out of thin air if none was presented to him. We would be in the office at 9 a.m. sharp and we did not know when we could leave for the day. If there was a banquet at Rashtrapati Bhavan, we had to be available in our room till 11 p.m. or till whenever the banquet got over. Work was tough but the President's office was a well-oiled machine and everything got done smoothly.

There are over 300 rooms in Rashtrapati Bhavan, but not all of them were for the President. One part was occupied by the cabinet secretariat; that was where bureaucracy's top man sat. He had perhaps a hundred rooms. The rest of the rooms were for the President and his secretariat and staff. His secretariat consisted of around a thousand, including directors, secretaries, deputy secretaries and under secretaries. Then there were the gardeners, the cooks, the attendants and so on.

The first floor had a library in the classic British style, with many vintage editions of novels and non-fiction in hardcover. In a corner was Kalam's bedroom overlooking the Mughal Garden. Each of the President's family members was entitled to a room. If Kalam had had a wife, she would have had her own room. In the family wing, Kalam took four halls, a study and a dining room. There was a family reception room too. The rooms and corridors were so large that the place exuded a kind of loneliness. Anyone staying there had to ring a bell to summon someone. The family wing had a separate kitchen. And the basement had a big kitchen, like a hotel kitchen. This would cater for the presidential dinners and banquets.

Among the administration, there was a controller to manage the household. Kalam's family kitchen had two attendants and was provided with all the facilities. He had one Telugu cook and one Tamil cook, as his regular food was south Indian. Kalam was a vegetarian from ever since anyone who knew him could remember. I vaguely remember someone telling me he ate meat till he was in the tenth standard and after that he did not even touch egg. His cooks were trained at a five-star hotel and were up to date with presidential etiquette. Just before the President hosted anyone, the household director would brief him on the use of cutlery and placements. He would listen, but he would not necessarily do things for the sake of protocol.

Whatever food Kalam ordered from the large kitchen for himself or for his personal visitors, he would pay for. The bill had to be presented to him at the end of every month by the controller. 'Don't tell me what happened in the past,' (that these bills were not paid by the President) he would say. We too had to pay for anything we ordered other than tea and coffee.

Kalam was extremely sensitive towards the staff. They were astounded at his concern for them and his curiosity about their work. Many gardeners, attendants and other subordinate staff have shared their surprise and happiness with me. We have never seen such a President, he is so nice, I would hear from time to time. He would chat with his security guards and attendants; he was not interested in maintaining the aura of his position among his staff. In the morning, he would come out for a walk and often chat with the gardener: Why does this flower have no fragrance? Why aren't there more birds visiting the garden? How do we attract more into the garden? And so on. The military staff (ADCs) that always accompanied him would translate for him, as Kalam did not speak Hindi and many of the staff could not follow English. He would then move towards the deer browsing in the woods of Rashtrapati Bhavan. One day in the peak of summer he was strolling in the garden when he noticed the security guards in their kiosks sweating away. Why can't you provide them fans in their booths, he asked the administration. Following that, every security kiosk was provided with fans in summer and heaters in winter.

After a week of Kalam's assuming office, the programmes and ceremonial functions began. The prime minister would come, foreign visitors began to visit and the banquets started, as did his trips to the various states. He announced his first destination – Godhra and Ahmedabad, which were still recovering from the riots earlier in 2002.

Many of his staff chorused in alarm, 'The government will not allow that.'

'Nothing doing, I will go to the place and visit the affected people,' he said. There was a commotion in official circles. The PMO would have to be told, and what would happen if the prime minister was not happy about this choice of the President's first destination for an official visit? Kalam was going to unnecessarily spark trouble.

The government relented to his request to visit Godhra. The last word came from Vajpayee: If he wants to go, let him go.

The Godhra visit was fixed for 12 August 2002. The public in Godhra thronged in large numbers to see him and greet him. Many came to him and cried. He met many common people. He did not make any comment on what had happened. I hated the place and did not want to go, but to accompany the President you have to know the nitty-gritties of his place of visit. It was a two-day visit, and he took a team of people, including academics, to find out how best to calm the situation. The chief minister of Gujarat accompanied Kalam throughout his visit.

Kalam's second trip was to Madhya Pradesh. 'Always, people in this position visit the cities. I want to visit a village. Find me a village where nobody of any position has visited so far.' We found a village close to Bhopal. Well, it was not so close, about 200 kilometres from the state capital. It had no roads, electricity or high school.

Once the President's trip is scheduled, for, say, 8 a.m., you have to be available by 7 a.m. or so. His retinue consisted of fifteen cars, first his, then the doctor's, then the military secretary's, then the private secretary's and so on. In his plane, he had a sitting room, bedroom, bathroom and dining area. We would be seated in the plane according to rank. As soon as the plane took off, he would ask, 'Where is that guy?' and I would go into his cabin, usually reserved for the family of the President, and brief him on his visit.

As per protocol, there would be a guard of honour to receive him, he would go to the Raj Bhavan at Bhopal, meet the governor there and leave for the village by helicopter. All of this was to happen with military precision, but Kalam would not stick to the usual formalities and mutual exchange of praise and respect with the governor and officials. He would want to know how the states were faring and about the economic situation. He would shoot questions to the district administration asking for various details of the districts. The senior officials would brief him. For them Kalam was not an ordinary President. He wasn't like other political figures who hardly professed any interest or raised questions about the state and its districts.

Part of the journey to this village in Madhya Pradesh was by helicopter and the rest by a muddy road. As we landed in a school ground in the village, we were shocked to see there was almost nothing there. The chief minister of the state accompanied Kalam throughout his visit. The President addressed the villagers in English, and a deputy collector translated for the crowd. The chief minister spoke in praise of Kalam.

It was a tribal school and the people looked extremely poor. One girl's voice piped up from the audience. 'We have school here only up to fourth standard.' Kalam turned to the chief minister, who was standing behind him. 'See what she is saying. To move to the next class, she has to travel 30 to 40 kilometres. Why can't you do something?'

The chief minister, a senior Congress leader, was a raja of that area, and it looked as if Kalam was going to outshine him. 'Don't worry, we are doing it,' replied the chief minister. He took the microphone from the girl and announced that the school would be upgraded to a high school from the very next month. 'Khush hai?' Two or three more announcements were made. One man said the village needed a bore well. That was also promised. The villagers who had gathered there, along with the police officers and heads of the state administration, stood in utter veneration observing the impact of the President's words.

Then Kalam said he wanted to go among the people and mingle with them. The police would not allow that, but he insisted on plunging into the crowd. The police then formed a kind of ring around him as he entered the crowd. Kalam shook every hand that was extended to him – it was a forest of hands.

It was always Kalam's desire to visit villages. As President, the security protocol made it difficult for him to go to remote villages. But there was something that beckoned him to them. His visit often helped make available certain facilities for those villages. He told me he chose to visit places with that purpose in mind. If a visit by the President of India is scheduled, the local government would be forced to arrange electricity if it was not there, get some roads tarred afresh and organize basic provisions. Once these things are brought in for the people, they cannot be taken back. A laid road cannot be rolled up and taken away, he would say. A similar visit was organized for him to Attapady, a tribal hamlet in Kerala, in November 2002.

Within a year he had visited all the states, and that was his target. He made it a particular point to visit the states in the North-East, where earlier presidents had rarely ventured. He visited all of them. Wherever he visited, the chief minister of the state would meet him, and there would be dinner and local cultural activities.

Kalam was particular about returning to Delhi as soon as his agenda was finished, whichever corner of India he was visiting. Later in the book we'll read about how he galvanized the Air Force into getting him back from the North-East to Delhi under what looked like impossible conditions. His reasoning was, 'If I stay even one extra hour, many people will have to remain on duty. Money will have to be spent. There will have to be police on the roads in Delhi if I land at some odd time.'

4

A Transformative President

My workload was heavy but work went on smoothly at the President's office, as I have said before. Many little things were new to me. I had to learn how to move with the President. One cannot walk abreast with him; one always had to keep a distance from him, falling a little behind. The ADCs assigned to his office would always walk with him.

As for Kalam, he may have been a figurehead as the President of India, but he never looked upon any work as a formality to quickly get out of the way or simply tick the boxes. There would be governors' appointments and judges' appointments that would come to him for approval. He would go through each of the papers. He would put his mind to the selection, and would check whether the candidate was eligible. In some cases, only his signature was required, not his opinion. Still, he would only sign the papers if the candidate was an eminent person; otherwise he would raise questions. He had to clear vice chancellor appointments of all central universities. He had to approve the transfer of governors. All new ambassadors and high commissioners had to present their credentials to the President. That was a formal function and he had to receive them. If a governor wanted a couple of days of casual leave, the President had to approve it.

Kalam was a late starter. He would come to the office only by 11 a.m. That was unusual for a man of his diligence. He would often have started work earlier though, in his residential rooms. There was a conference in Bangalore, an international conference, where his presence was scheduled from 9.30 to 10.30 a.m. But Kalam emerged from his room only at 9.30 a.m. I had to inform security about the delay as roads have to be blocked well in advance for his travel. Somebody wrote him an email once: 'Your movement is delaying our work. I have lost one casual leave because of it.' I told Kalam about it. He was otherwise very sensitive about inconveniencing the public, but he seemed helpless in this matter. Later he apologized to the individual for the inconvenience. He said he had a big problem; he needed four hours to get ready. 'You schedule things accordingly,' he told me.

So, for a 9 a.m. meeting I had to ensure he woke up at 5.15 a.m. He would have tea and some biscuits over the day's newspapers. That would take about twenty minutes. Then he would spend half an hour on his shaving. After which he would clean his dentures. Naturally, his face would look different and he would not open the door for anyone until they were cleaned and put on again. Only an attendant could enter. He also spent a lot of time setting his hair, as I was to discover later. In his early presidential days, all this would happen relatively briskly, but later he became very slow.

Breakfast was at around 11 a.m., lunch at 4 p.m. and dinner between 10 p.m. and 11 p.m. The attendants could not retire for the day till the President finished his dinner. There was a complaint about this, and it was solved by putting the attendants in shifts. Once dinner was ready, it only had to be served. And for that you needed only one man who had to remain there till 1 a.m.

Retired Major General R. Swaminathan, a person well known to Kalam, had been appointed as officer on special duty (OSD) in late 2003. Swaminathan would often sit with him at the dinner table, discussing the next day's programme and points to include in his speech. If there was, say, an international electronics conference where Kalam was invited to speak, Swaminathan would be asked to dig up interesting bits of information. Kalam did not want to say the usual banal things in his speeches or simply read out the draft speeches provided by the concerned ministries or departments, which is the usual practice. He wanted to say something that would engage his audience or even amaze it, whether the listeners were experts in electronics or in agriculture.

Similarly, whichever community or state Kalam addressed, he would say something unexpected and often greet the public in their language. As a speaker or chief guest, he always made it a point to make his speech a hit. The community and organizers would be left feeling that the President had spoken to them personally and had given them an agenda for change. Some leaders now follow Kalam's style. He could hardly be an expert in so many fields, but the truth was he knew how to present an idea. He would not simply read out a speech or make a rote presentation, and if somebody asked him a question, he would respond with as meaningful an answer as possible. Therefore, politicians, even if they were popular, did not like to share the stage with him, as he always stole the show. As a result, they did not invite him for public functions if they could help it, though sometimes protocol made it unavoidable. In my observation, the political leaders from his own state of Tamil Nadu were most sensitive to this. To me, it seemed that the two stalwarts of Tamil Nadu politics were wary of him and ensured that they or their ministers never shared the dais with him during his visits to the state as former president. Of course, for such events as the celebration of 150 years of Madras University, Kalam had to be invited.

Occasionally, he addressed the state legislatures when he visited state capitals. There was one such talk planned in Tamil Nadu, but it was dropped at the instance of the top leadership. But in Kerala, he was very popular. Every member of the Legislative Assembly (MLA) turned up to hear him irrespective of party affiliation. Whether it was left leaders or the Congress, all of them happily welcomed him and they considered it an honour to share the dais with Kalam.

I recall an MLA requesting me for a meeting with Kalam at the airport so that he could touch his hand. He pleaded with me and drove all the way from Idukki to Kochi airport for a short visit. He reached just before the President's flight was to take off. I arranged the meeting and the MLA thanked me profusely for the one-minute meeting and for being able to touch the President.

Kalam gave Kerala a vision document, outlining possibilities for employment generation and tourism based on the state's economic strengths. Oommen Chandy, the chief minister, announced the formation of a team of officials immediately after Kalam's address to the state legislature. The team was asked to study and report on the vision document and its possible implementation. One of Kalam's suggestions to the state was to activate a smart waterway from Kasaragod to Thiruvananthapuram, thereby reducing transportation load by road. Though he followed up with the Kerala chief minister, it yielded no result.

Once on a Delhi–Thiruvananthapuram flight Kalam spotted V.S. Achuthanandan, chief minister of Kerala from 2006 to 2011, and went up to his seat in the economy class and sat with him for 15–20 minutes to discuss the progress of the work on the waterway. Later, on what happened to be his last visit to the state, in May 2015, just a couple of months before his demise, he again told the then chief minister about his dream of a smart waterway connecting Kerala from one end to the other. Nothing came of it.

Every time Kalam was invited to a programme, our workload doubled. Major General Swaminathan's entry into our team was a great relief for me and the others. We had to collect material from the relevant departments, and Swaminathan and two or three others would collate the material for Kalam's speech. Everyone in the office was involved. Sometimes drafts were distributed to those close to Kalam, and five or six pairs of eyes would go through the document before it was finalized. This kind of preparation was so much more rigorous than anything politicians would do. As I said before, they resented Kalam's popularity among the common people. Everybody knew him. He was the people's president. Even the Congress chief did not seem to like him. Only Prime Minister Vajpayee appeared to be unfazed by his popularity.

There were the foreign trips to do, of course. Kalam had to go on several reciprocal visits. His first overseas visit was in late 2003 to the UAE, Sudan and Bulgaria. In the UAE, his agenda was to address the Indian community and the chamber of commerce. He met the President of the UAE. These were high-level visits. In Khartoum he met the President of Sudan and told him India could help them in the education sector through the pan-African e-network. He often departed from the material that was prepared for him by external affairs ministry. He would try to use his influence with the DRDO and the ISRO to follow up and get things moving.

Kalam infused into the President's office a new energy and enthusiasm like never before. The office was equipped with the latest technology with induction of new computers and other electronic devices like the latest printers and scanners. Kalam was very keen to tap the potential of information technology (IT) to make his engagements with the people easier, both for himself and for them. He even set up an IT interface system so people could communicate with him easily.

My primary duty at Rashtrapati Bhavan was to handle the innumerable emails and letters that came every day for Kalam. I had to go through each of them and sort them out according to the seriousness of the matter, and present a selection to him at the daily evening meeting set up for this. During Kalam's tenure, the number of requests, complaints and memorandums received from the public increased tremendously. Everybody took the liberty to write to the President about any and every grievance they had. The matters ranged from violence at home to installation of street lights and issue of ration cards by local governments. School students, senior citizens, housewives, autorickshaw drivers, all kinds of people wrote to him. Kalam considered all of them seriously and replied to many with gravity. A number of small requests were passed on straight to the district magistrates or district collectors of the concerned regions instead of routing them through the concerned central ministries.

I would read out the gist of each letter and Kalam would act in a flash, often immediately contacting the concerned state government or the district collector. Often, because the request came from the President, this resulted in immediate action, and replies from the local offices reporting compliance followed. There prevailed an impression among district collectors across the country that Kalam's forwarding a letter to them meant the issue raised was of significance and urgency. Kalam was astute enough to forward only genuine complaints, and the recipient authorities found it gratifying to act on them. Of course, sometimes it was with total discomfiture that the bureaucracy abided by his instructions.

Often, there would be a flood of requests praying for his intervention. When the number of such letters became inordinately large, we were forced to keep aside those that appeared to be of comparatively less significance. Letters received from girls and women were given utmost priority. Many girls wrote to him, pleading that the President intervene to defer their marriage until they completed their education. The President would immediately instruct one of his advisers to communicate with the parents. It was sad that a large number of complaints were from women subjected to domestic violence. There was a feeling among the people that once their voice reached Rashtrapati Bhavan, their problems would somehow be solved.

Kalam loved to have people directly communicate with him. Every time there was a public interaction, especially with children or youth, he would ask them to write to him, dictating to them his email ID. As a consequence, his official website, www.presidentofindia.nic.in, was an interactive platform that allowed people to write directly to the President. People from remote and poor areas used to write to him on whatever scraps of paper they could find. During my five years at Rashtrapati Bhavan, I saw letters written on shabby pieces of paper and sheets ripped out of notebooks, sent by farmers, students and housewives.

One letter I recall clearly was from a public-minded person who wrote to the President asking him to come to the aid of three old unmarried sisters suffering from illness, living in a dangerously dilapidated house in a place called Athavanadu in Kerala. The news appeared in a local daily and was forwarded to the President. On seeing it, Kalam immediately pressed the buzzer to call me. When I went to his room, he asked me where Athavanadu was in Kerala. I had no clue, and the Secretary to the President, P.M. Nair, also from Kerala, did not know either. I placed a call to my father, who was at the time bedridden with Parkinson's. Still, he was fully alert and clear mentally. He told me the place was in Malappuram district. Within ten minutes, I passed on the information to Kalam, who immediately instructed the district collector of Malappuram, M. Sivasanker, to urgently look up the women. The district collector took immediate steps to relocate the ladies to a safe house and the necessary support was provided to them using government resources.

One year, President Kalam decided to interact with the postmen of the country. He had a great fondness for the India Post as letters had been his only means of communication with the outside world during his early days in Rameswaram. About 150 postmen from across the country were invited to visit Rashtrapati Bhavan. In his address to them he told them how important they were, how they were the link between the common man of poor means and the outside world. He showered praise on them. It was such a morale booster for the postmen; they left Rashtrapati Bhavan with their hearts brimming. No one else would have honoured them in such a manner.

It was Kalam who also first invited panchayat heads and gram sevaks to Rashtrapati Bhavan, a practice which continues to this day. They were offered a grand reception and felicitation. He talked to them about the need for grassroots development and their place in the nation's scheme of things. The central university vice chancellors' meet, a regular event now, was also Kalam's idea. It was a three-day meet during Kalam's tenure. Kalam recharged the vice chancellors, sharing with them his innovative ideas and vision for the country. He also insisted on follow-up and feedback after these meetings.

Diwali day was open house at Rashtrapati Bhavan. Anybody could visit that day to wish him. By

10–10.30 a.m., there would be thousands queued up in the garden. One year I counted 3,000. They would come to shake hands with the President and maybe get a photo taken with him. That was all. Some would bring their children to be blessed by him. Few presidents before or since met common people the same way; they would view visitors from the window. I think it must have been a record, the President shaking the hands of thousands of visitors in a day at Rashtrapati Bhavan. During Eid, rather than celebrating it at Rashtrapati Bhavan, Kalam would donate the funds to yatimkhanas.

People ranging from cooks to CEOs visited Kalam. Some would come with gifts, but the gifts would be returned. Flowers were accepted. Many people were afraid to enter because of the formidable security at the gates. Only the bolder ones ventured in. But even they were in the thousands. People would come from across the country to visit him. The President would shake hands with everyone, from the first to the last person in the queue. People visited on Kalam's birthday, on Eid, and on New Year's Day too. On those days, the President would be available to shake hands with all from 11 a.m. to 3 p.m. Some minister would drop by in between and he would break the queue to greet him.

Kalam did not like to stay away from people. He wanted Rashtrapati Bhavan to be made more and more accessible to ordinary citizens. They should be able to see the ninety-year-old 340-room building set in 5 acres in a 330-acre plot, he said. A letter he got questioning the need for such extravagant accommodation for the country's President may have prompted these thoughts. Finally, it was decided that Rashtrapati Bhavan would be open for the public on certain days. Currently, it is open for public visitors three days a week. Kalam also created a unique exhibition to inspire children who visited the building. India's proud achievements in the field of science were well displayed there. During his period there was no entry fee for visitors, and there was a tremendous rush of people visiting Rashtrapati Bhavan in Kalam's time. Later, some regulations were imposed to help manage the growing number of visitors.

Religious leaders also called on Kalam at Rashtrapati Bhavan. One such was the Shankaracharya of Kanchi Kamakoti, who visited Kalam before the controversy around the matha. He was accompanied by his devotee Swaminathan, an Iyer from Thanjavur. The Shankaracharya sat in the sofa in the visitors' room and was there for about an hour and a half. He was given a warm welcome and received properly with a purna kumbha. Employees who were his devotees were permitted to meet him.

Mata Amritanandamayi was another such visitor. Kalam held her in high regard. She would often visit

Delhi to meet her devotees, and her ashram had requested the meeting. She spent half a day at Rashtrapati Bhavan, spending some time in Kalam's office and in the garden, where she was shown the deer and peacocks. Sri Sri Ravishankar, Christian bishops and Muslim clergy too paid visits. Sai Baba of Puttaparthi had given President Kalam a watch, which he did not wear. Later the Sai Baba sent word asking if he wore it and then I saw it on him.

Music was an obsession with Kalam, especially Carnatic music. Many musicians were invited to Rashtrapati Bhavan to perform in the in-house theatre for a select audience. Violinist L. Subramaniam, singer Kavita Krishnamurthy and drummer Sivamani were among the many artistes who performed on the Rashtrapati Bhavan lawns or in the small auditorium in the complex. Ustad Bismillah Khan gave one of his last performances, cut short as he was unable to play any further after a short spell on the shehnai. The entire staff of Rashtrapati Bhavan was invited to these cultural performances, irrespective of their seniority, unlike in the time of later presidents. Such occasions were a matter of great happiness for the staff, because for the first time a president was not considering hierarchy to put together the guest list for an event. Even gardeners and other workers took pride in publicly saying 'I'm a staff of Kalam's'. There would be guests from outside too at these concerts. Delhi residents generally do not care about who occupies Rashtrapati Bhavan as president. But Kalam was different. In that sense he broke the glass ceiling. He opened the majestic estate of the first citizen of India for viewing to all classes of citizens.

He was especially interested in gardening. To maintain the Mughal Garden in the way it deserved, he demanded the services of a horticulturist. In due course the DRDO provided a scientist and Kalam and he planned for an herb garden at Rashtrapati Bhavan. Soon a number of pots containing sprightly saplings arrived in the garden. Initially the rigid bureaucracy at Rashtrapati Bhavan were averse to the idea and tried to create hurdles. An herbal wing in the garden of Rashtrapati Bhavan ought not to be among the priorities of the country's President, they felt. But it was not an ordinary President's ambition. It was Kalam's dream, and it naturally became a reality.

When it came to family though, Kalam appeared wary of entertaining them in his official capacity. He was very close to them, and around fifteen members of his family arrived by the Grand Trunk Express from Tamil Nadu for the swearing-in. I was assigned to receive them. I knew only his brother's daughter, the only member of his family with whom I had interacted when Kalam was in the defence ministry. None of us knew the rest of the family. A minivan was hired to bring them from the station. I informed the stationmaster, and the Indian Railways had also arranged a reception for them. They were very modest and unassuming and wore south Indian attire and chappals. The train was brought to platform no. 1, as it is when important people are arriving. A big retinue of media was waiting outside. His family had been warned not to talk to them. There was always the possibility that someone might shoot off his or her mouth. Kalam would not like that at all.

The family was taken to the guest house from the station. They all attended the swearing-in, confining themselves to one corner. Kalam spent an hour with them that day, showing them around Rashtrapati Bhavan. But after lunch he kind of packed them away. They were to take a train back the same night. Go with them and see them off, he told me. They had been waitlisted on the return journey, but of course the Indian Railways confirmed their reservation. They were the family of the first citizen. All fifteen were accommodated in one bogie, and an Indian Railways officer was assigned to look after their needs on their journey from Delhi to Chennai. I waited till 10.30 p.m. for the train to leave. Kalam had given money to cover his family's food expenses at the rail pantry. After they were seen off we had to report to the President that all went well.

Kalam was not a president who adhered to protocol. There was a strict security cordon that prohibited him from venturing beyond certain limits, especially into crowds, wherever he went, but he wanted to be a free bird. So whenever he found the protocols too rigid and restrictive, he would breach them. As it is, he was excited about meeting people, and then the people's frenzy to get close to him would feed his excitement further. Without any warning he would go beyond barricades to mingle with the crowds.

I was witness to this several times. Given the stature of his office, the security personnel were afraid to do or say anything in public to control his movements. Sometimes they would turn to me to persuade him to restrain himself. 'Sir, no, you can't go beyond this point,' I would say. But he would not listen, as the spell of the masses threw him into a different mood. 'No, no, no. You come, you come with me,' he would tell his security guys. Well, if the President ordered, the security people had to obey. Still, I would warn him of possible mobbing, commotion and stampede. But he would not listen, especially if he saw children, youth and mothers, whom he liked to chat with. Sometimes children held on to his hand and took the pen from his shirt pocket, and he would enjoy all this. Youngsters of all ages loved him – from pre-primary children who didn't know who exactly he was to IIT students. They would go close to

Kalam, reaching out to shake hands with him, and take photos with him. The security personnel would often complain to me about not preventing such scenes. Little did they know that these matters were well beyond my control. Thankfully, nothing untoward ever happened because of Kalam's stepping over his security cordon.

Security was only one aspect of Kalam's love of crowd adulation. His keenness to keep mingling with people sometimes affected his schedule and return journey to Delhi, especially when it was by helicopter. Many remote venues do not have regular airports but only facilities for a chopper to land. Very often this meant getting to the nearest airport and going by chopper to the venue. Whenever Kalam had evening programmes, the district collectors and other officials would become tense. His long interactions with the people would hamper on-time movement of his helicopter. Once in Saharanpur in Uttar Pradesh, after a grand function, Kalam in his characteristic style breached protocol and began to interact with the children and the youth among the audience. Officials began persuading him to leave. Their anxiety was that a helicopter could not take off after 6 p.m. with a VIP passenger. Kalam ignored them and continued to chat with the crowd pleasantly. Time passed, and soon it was past six. Now his helicopter could not take off. The only options were for the President's team to stay the night there and travel to the nearest airport by helicopter the next day or to proceed to the airport by road that evening. Kalam would not stay overnight at a place unless it was unavoidable. So he chose to reach the nearby airport by road. Now there was another grave issue. To be taken to the airport, his entourage required twenty cars, and we were in a small hilly village. Arranging for these many cars was not an easy task. However, the district collector was resourceful and mustered enough vehicles. When the cars were ready, there was still another issue. They didn't have enough fuel for travelling up to the airport, which was quite a distance away. So refuelling was arranged along the route, and the convoy stopped at a fuel station along the way. The President's car also needed refuelling. Security protocol required that the President not sit inside the vehicle while it was fuelling, and Kalam had to wait outside the petrol pump in a public place cordoned off by his security. Once the vehicles were refuelled, the convoy started crawling to the airport, where the President's chartered flight was waiting. When we reached the airport, it was 9 p.m.

Kalam's insistence on immediately returning to Delhi after an event from anywhere in India, and even from overseas if it was possible, was mainly to avoid burdening state governments with arrangements for his stay and security. He was frugal with his spending and did not want to burden the nation's exchequer for his extra stay anywhere. He avoided all unnecessary travel, sightseeing and shopping, whether domestic or international. He was highly sensitive that there should be no negative news reports about the President going sightseeing or on pleasure trips. So, once the official engagements were finished, President Kalam and crew would immediately return from wherever they were. Of course, it did not strike him that this insistence could inconvenience the country's administration in other ways.

On a visit to Mizoram, an extraordinary incident took place in Aizawl. Kalam's programme was over in the evening, and after the official dinner hosted by the governor, the President as usual wanted to fly back to Delhi that very night. According to the protocol-approved schedule, the President and his entourage had to stay that night in Aizawl and depart the next morning at ten after breakfast. Kalam was of the opinion that the night stay at Aizawl would serve no purpose. Once the dinner and programmes hosted jointly by the chief minister and the governor were over, President Kalam summoned the military secretary, who had already retired to his room. He asked him to arrange for his return flight to Delhi, much to the shock of the man and his team.

Aizawl airport did not have night take-off facilities like runway lights, and was operational only up to

3 p.m. The military secretary, after talking the matter over with Air Force officials, told the President that it was not possible to leave for Delhi that night as there were no night take-off facilities, and the only option was to leave early the next day. I was with the President while this briefing happened. The military secretary's explanation did not satisfy the President. In fact, he got irritated and asked, 'If there is a war tomorrow, what will you do? Can you say that you can't take off since there is no night take-off and we will fight only the next day?'

The flabbergasted military secretary immediately obtained permission from the chief of air staff for take-off facilities to be arranged at Aizawl airport. Things then progressed on a war footing. In no time the Air Force station was abuzz. All the personnel were asked to report for duty. The entire stretch of the runway was lit along the rims with kerosene lamps. By 10.30 p.m., the two Avro aircraft that would carry the President and his team were ready to fly. Kerosene lamps flickered along the runway, showing the aircraft the way forward, and slowly we were lifted into the dark sky twinkling with stars. The journey carried an extra high risk, for it was unusual for a flying machine to venture into the skies between Aizawl and Guwahati in the dark in a landscape surrounded by hills. We landed at Guwahati airport at around 11.30 p.m. There the President's Boeing aircraft was waiting for us. Apart from office and private space for the President, the aircraft also had facilities to seat the President's entourage. We landed in Delhi a few hours later, as per the wish of President Kalam.

Kalam had created a lot of avoidable trouble, possibly causing more administrative strain and expense (exactly what he said he wanted to avoid) than if he had stayed overnight at Aizawl. But on second thoughts, he did put to test the resourcefulness of the military and the bureaucracy, jolting them out of their routine and ensuring that they were on their toes. And they did rise to the occasion.

5

A Second Term?

I have described Kalam as a man utterly devoted to work, not given to any personal indulgences and supremely particular about not misusing his office, paying up for any expense that he felt was personal. It might be surprising then that such a man had enemies, or, let us say, people who did not like him. I put that down to two reasons: one, that Kalam, though apolitical, refused to be a puppet President; and two, that he outshone most politicians at any public forum, which they utterly resented.

As the end of his term neared, there was overwhelming public opinion in favour of his continuing in office. He got thousands of letters and emails from across the country telling him he had to continue as President, that he was the person everyone loved and so on. He also got letters from several eminent people asking him to continue in office. I still have one such letter from the eminent jurist Fali Nariman asking him not to refuse an offer of a second term. A lot of the correspondence of that time relating to this is in the possession of his family. The media too seemed to be of the opinion that he should continue.

There was a strong rumour that some politicians too wanted him to continue. He had become President during the reign of the BJP-led NDA, and now it was the Congress-led UPA ruling at the Centre. Some among the Congress wanted him to continue, but not so their supreme leader. There were those who did not want him to continue, as they felt that he was holding up some senior Congress leader's chance at the post. But soon there were clear feelers being sent out to him to test his readiness for a second term.

Gradually, the media got a whiff of this and, of course, started digging around for opinions and comments to find out if he was indeed under consideration. The leader of one of the left parties supporting the UPA from outside made things very clear when he told the media that the presidential candidate would not be decided by emails and messages – a dig at the correspondence Kalam was receiving exhorting him to continue, news of which seemed to have got around to the media.

Since Kalam's association with the Pokhran-II blasts, the left had not been in his favour. The other thing that irked them was a random comment Kalam made in one of his speeches as President that India should have a two-party system, and that smaller parties should merge into one party or the other.

Of course, there were individual politicians from the left who liked him. Like Binoy Vishwam of the Communist Party of India (CPI), who rushed from Idukki to Kochi during one of Kalam's visits to Kerala, and was content to just hold his hand and exchange greetings with him. But politically he had to follow his party's views.

The CPI's general secretary A.B. Bardhan, a severe critic of Kalam's, did not share Vishwam's reverence for the President; they made a strong pitch for Pratibha Patil. 'We will show Kalam how a President ought to behave' was the message their comments and actions conveyed. They were completely against Kalam's proactive role as President.

So, suddenly, Mrs Patil was announced as the UPA's presidential candidate. Kalam read about these developments and comments in the newspapers, but would simply smile and say nothing. Close to demitting office, he became yogi-like. He had always been that way, but I felt he became even more so as time passed. You could criticize him, blame him, say anything, but no response at all would be forthcoming from him.

There were at least two instances, according to me, when Kalam could have managed a second term as President had he been ready for some quid pro quo politics. A couple of months before he was to demit office, the Dravida Munnetra Kazhagam (DMK) patriarch called on him. He had a good number of MPs at that time and told Kalam he could tilt the decision in his favour. However, nothing came of their discussion.

He was soon followed by the supreme leader of the All India Anna Dravida Munnetra Kazhagam (AIADMK). Her party was in opposition in Tamil Nadu at that time, and she pleaded with Kalam to contest for a second term as a candidate of the Third Front. That would have created a big problem for the largest party at the Centre, and they were already nervous about this possibility as there were many disgruntled insiders who may have voted for Kalam and not the Congress's candidate. And the AIADMK leader seemed determined to work against the Congress, which was then aligned with her arch-rival. I was told that she made a very strong pitch while trying to persuade Kalam to contest. She promised to gather all the opposition parties to vote for him. But Kalam was firm – if there was no consensus, he would not contest, he said. So, she too, like her rival, left his office dejected by his decision not to contest.

Until May (Kalam's tenure was to end in July 2007), there was a rumour floating about that Kalam's candidature was not ruled out. Then came the sudden announcement by the UPA of their choice of Pratibha Patil. Perhaps they did not want a President with a public face and public support; they did not like it that a President had become so popular. However, even though the UPA and the left supported Patil, if Kalam had tried hard he may have fetched comparable support, but then he wanted to be liked by all. I strongly felt that he would have liked to continue but did not want to risk a defeat. That was one weakness of his, perhaps – that he wanted constant assurance that he was liked and respected by all. He was afraid of criticism of any kind and tried his best to avoid controversy. He also feared that people might call him power-hungry, someone who wanted to stick on to his seat. In 2002 he had had the support of 80 per cent of the political leaders. Now, in 2007, he was not too sure and did not want to jump into the fray if he was not assured one hundred per cent success.

Among those who were not in favour of Kalam was the Congress chief. It was believed that Kalam did not discourage questions that were raised about her Indian citizenship after she emerged victorious in the 2004 elections and the Congress wanted her to become prime minister. In his memoirs Kalam has written that he received a large amount of correspondence from both individuals and institutions questioning her citizenship status and that he had passed them on to the relevant agencies. In *Turning Points: A Journey through Challenges*, Kalam wrote:

> During this time there were many political leaders who came to meet me to request me not to succumb to any pressure and appoint Mrs Gandhi as the Prime Minister, a request that would not have been constitutionally tenable. If she had made any claim for herself I would have had no option but to appoint her.

It does appear that Kalam was not a walkover and wanted due process to be followed but the Congress leader considered this as his doubting her credentials to become prime minister (whether she wanted to or not). Kalam never said anything openly about her citizenship, but somehow I got the impression that everything about what he did and did not do at the time indicated that he felt she could not become prime minister. That must have been relayed to her or was sensed by her.

There was another episode that alienated him from the Congress chief even more. In 2006 the government moved an ordinance to redefine 'office of profit'. Kalam returned the Office of Profit Bill which exempted certain offices of state and central governments – including the National Advisory Council (NAC) headed by Sonia Gandhi – from the purview of office of profit for MPs, but when the UPA sent it back unchanged, he signed it.

As an MP, the Congress chief could not hold any office of profit. So this ordinance was widely perceived as a move to save her from disqualification as an MP. A mighty furore erupted, and many political parties – the BJP and the Samajwadi Party in the forefront – petitioned the President for her disqualification as an MP.

Kalam's attitude towards whatever files the government sent him was to keep them and examine them. He would not just mechanically sign them and send them on. An MP could hold only one post in the government. The Congress chief was UPA chairperson and NAC chairman. As per the rule, she could not hold so many posts. She had to resign either as MP or as NAC head. It was because of Kalam's adamancy that the ordinance was put on hold.

The Congress chief responded by dramatically resigning as both MP and NAC chief, and for some time she was not an MP till she got re-elected. That she felt Kalam did not take her side was evident when Rahul Gandhi came to meet Kalam. He was closeted with the President for a full hour. That was the only time I saw Rahul Gandhi meeting Kalam. The next time I saw him was at Kalam's funeral in Rameswaram, travelling in a special aircraft all alone nine years later to show the nation that they were not against Kalam. To go back to the meeting, once Rahul Gandhi left the room, I asked Kalam, 'Sir, why has he suddenly come?' Kalam gave me some ridiculous explanation, but was smiling broadly. 'He wanted my guidance,' was all he told me. Definitely, there had been some tough talk behind those closed doors that day.

But Kalam's quiet projection of himself as an upright person, and perhaps the only one for miles around, really annoyed many people. In fact, during the last few years of his life, whenever he addressed crowds, he would goad them with some stirring question, whose answer by implication was 'You [Kalam] are the only honest/righteous man.' One day I was told by someone close to the Congress leadership, 'Please tell your boss that our chief too is not from a political background and is very honest.' I avoided conveying such messages to Kalam. Kalam loved to project himself as someone no one could point fingers at. Of course, he never openly said all this, but his speeches and the way he led conversations make that clear.

All this must have irked the Congress chief. Had he been on good terms with her, he would definitely have been supported for a second term. From my observations and calculations, this dislike was mutual. Kalam was not for the Congress or the BJP. But he did like Vajpayee very much and always visited him to wish him on his birthday till the last year of his life.

It is to Kalam's credit that despite these run-ins with the Congress chief he was gracious enough to extend help to the Congress and lent a hand in preventing the fall of UPA-I. The government was in a critical condition and was seeking a vote of confidence over the India–US nuclear treaty, the seeds of which had been sown in 2005 between President George Bush and Manmohan Singh. The left would clearly not vote for it, having ideological problems with the deal. But Mulayam Singh Yadav, the Samajwadi Party chief, whose support was critical for the government, was not entirely convinced about the deal either. Finally, Mulayam agreed that if Kalam said the deal was good for India, he would support the government. Kalam was no longer President and had moved to a house he had been provided on Rajaji Marg. Mulayam visited him there and discussed the deal with him. Kalam told him the deal would be good for India and that the country should proceed with it. When Mulayam emerged from the meeting, he had decided to support the deal, and the government survived. Still, the Congress chief neither visited nor called on Kalam to acknowledge the good turn he had done her government. Of course, to be fair to her, she had never requested him to speak in support of the deal either. But then, Manmohan Singh soon visited him at his house to personally thank him, perhaps on his chief's instructions.

Around this time, Kalam was severely criticized for his knowledge and role as a scientist. A former DRDO scientist, K. Santhanam, claimed that Pokhran-II had not been a complete success. Santhanam was backed by Homi Sethna, who had led the Pokhran-I test in 1974. Another former chief of the Atomic Energy Commission, P.K. Iyengar, was also of the view that the Pokhran-II tests were shoddily done on the orders of an impatient government. Kalam simply kept quiet through all this. I think his saving of UPA-I had brought him back into the limelight, which the old veterans possibly found hard to digest.

After the 2009 elections, it was UPA-II in power. With a group of around thirty-five MPs, the DMK had bargained for good portfolios and got them too. Things were moving smoothly at the Centre. A few ministers of UPA-II were friendly with Kalam. For example, Jairam Ramesh, the minister for environment and forests, suddenly declared that kids from all over India had chosen Dr A.P.J. Abdul Kalam as 'Bharat ka Paryavaran Ambassador' or 'India's ambassador for the environment'. A.K. Antony, when he took over as defence minister, visited Kalam at his home because of the old friendship and sought guidance on his new ministry. But after that day he never showed up. Apart from these politicians, generally the UPA ministers kept their distance from him. Perhaps there was a tacit understanding to do so.

Somehow, it was ensured that Congress leaders kept away from Kalam. In 2011, when the nation was reeling under various corruption scandals that were being reported every other day – the Commonwealth Games scandal and the 2G and coal 'scams' – Kalam was disturbed at the developments and asked us to connect him to Prime Minister Manmohan Singh. Within no time the prime minister called back. Kalam told the prime minister he wanted to discuss some issues of national importance with him at his place. Manmohan Singh immediately responded with a 'Yes, of course'. But instead of Kalam visiting his office, he would come over to Kalam's residence, he assured him. Kalam was happy that the prime minister had responded positively to his request. But the visit was not to be. Manmohan Singh never made it, despite several reminders sent to his office. We were told later he allegedly could not get the approval of his leader for the meeting. This happened again the next year. I must have spent a whole day making those telephone calls to Singh's office. The prime minister was simply not permitted to meet Kalam. A meeting would of course have set the rumour mills ringing. There would be speculations on the meeting, and a press statement or conference may have had to be held to clarify what the meeting was about. There would have been ramifications.

Even as former president, Kalam continued to outshine the political leaders of the day. The big event in the country in 2010 was the Commonwealth Games, which was hosted by India. Kalam was one of the invitees for the inaugural function held at the Jawaharlal Nehru Stadium at New Delhi. One by one, as the dignitaries came in, their names would be announced and their entries were met with feeble applause from the crowd of more than 50,000 people assembled at the stadium. There were the prime minister, the sitting president and some significant others, including the Congress chief, in the VIP area. But when Kalam's name was announced and he entered, the crowd exploded in applause, some even calling out his name aloud. None of the dignitaries there would have failed to note this.

As I have mentioned before, the most intense dislike he fetched seemed to be from the leaders of his own home state. Kalam, who could speak fluent Tamil, was a particular draw in his state. People were drawn by the way he made presentations and speeches – first, he took the trouble to say something of relevance, and second, even if he were not an expert in the subject at hand, he would somehow find a way to answer any question thrown at him. On the dais anywhere, he outshone most politicians of that time and people were keener to listen to him than to the politicians. The crowd would slowly disperse once his speech was over. That irked many of them. Plus, he would be mobbed for handshakes, photographs and autographs while the other VIPs were largely ignored, which hurt many of them. Many states, including Karnataka, Andhra Pradesh, Chhattisgarh, Bihar and Kerala, would invite him when they had important state programmes, but in Tamil Nadu he was never invited to any functions if the government could help it. But protocol sometimes required that he be called, such as when Madras University celebrated its 150th anniversary. None of the Tamil Nadu ministers, whether they belonged to the DMK or the AIADMK, would share the dais with Kalam, apparently so as not to invite the wrath of their party chiefs.

Once Kalam received a request to address the inmates of Puzhal Central Prison, the largest jail in Tamil Nadu. At that time Karunanidhi was the chief minister of the state and Kalam was no longer president. The letter was from the prison's director general (DGP). I showed the communication to Kalam, and I too was enthused by the invite to meet and address the inmates of a large prison. Kalam instantly approved the request. As was his habit, once he agreed to attend a function, he earnestly set about preparing his speech. He put in a lot of effort and conceived a nice speech for the occasion. But on the eve of the event, I received a phone call

Sondeep Shankar, Getty Images

A.P.J. Abdul Kalam, then Scientific Adviser to the Defence Minister, at the launch of the Main Battle Tank, January 1996

Wikimedia Commons

President Kalam addressing the nation on the eve of Independence Day, 14 August 2004

Wikimedia Commons

President Kalam interacting with students of various schools of New Delhi at Rashtrapati Bhavan on the eve of Republic Day, 25 January 2007

Wikimedia Commons

President Kalam greeting Prime Minister Vajpayee on his 79th birthday in New Delhi, 25 December 2003

The India Today Group, Getty Images

He took delight in nature. Here at the Mughal Garden, Rashtrapati Bhavan, February 2007

The India Today Group, Getty Images

Inspecting a guard of honour at Rashtrapati Bhavan

The India Today Group, Getty Images

The President with the Prime Minister: A.P.J. Abdul Kalam and Manmohan Singh

The India Today Group, Getty Images

The President, the Prime Minister and the UPA chairperson, Sonia Gandhi, at the 136th birth anniversary of Mahatma Gandhi, October 2005

Manan Vatsyayana, Getty Images

President Kalam with spiritual leaders Sri Sri Ravishankar and H.H. the Dalai Lama

The India Today Group, Getty Images

Greeting guests at Rashtrapati Bhavan. In his tenure, Rashtrapati Bhavan became accessible to the people in a way it never was before.

Author's personal collection

President Kalam with R.K. Prasad, who was his private secretary from 1993

Author's personal collection

President Kalam with staff: (*From the left*) R.K. Prasad, Maj. Gen. Vinod Chopra (Military Secretary) and V. Ponraj (Director, TI)

Prakash Singh, Getty Images

The new President Pratibha Patil and the outgoing President A.P.J. Abdul Kalam, 25 July 2007

Pacific Press, Getty Images

Former president Kalam talks with students in Allahabad, November 2014. If anything, his popularity soared after he demitted office.

Photo Section, Rashtrapati Bhavan

Former president Kalam with Prime Minister Narendra Modi

Indranil Mukherjee, Getty Images

A nation grieves. Students hold vigil in memory of the former president on 28 July 2015

from the DGP saying that 'due to certain unexpected reasons' the programme had been cancelled. I told him that a mere phone call would not do and that he would have to send a formal communication for the record. In a short while, we received an email from the DGP announcing cancellation of the next day's event. Kalam was a bit upset and irritated at this last-minute cancellation. However, he responded in his usual cool-headed way. Later, through some reliable sources who requested anonymity, I found out that the DMK chief had put a spoke in the wheel. Apparently the DGP hadn't taken approval from the chief minister's office before inviting Kalam.

During Kalam's presidency, invitations from Tamil Nadu came only if protocol demanded it, and during the eight years of his life after his presidency there was not a single invitation extended to him by the Tamil Nadu government. He never expressed his displeasure at this. But right next door, in Kerala, he was in great demand, as I have mentioned earlier. For instance, in May 2015 when Kalam visited Kochi to inaugurate a superspeciality hospital, Aster Medicity, all of Kerala's cabinet ministers led by the CM were present to receive him. Even Karnataka and Andhra Pradesh would frequently invite him over for programmes, and often the chief ministers themselves would write to him.

As for Jayalalithaa, she did not even receive him, which is the custom, when, after demitting his office of President, he flew to Chennai on the evening of 25 July 2007. In fact, there was an incident that clearly indicated to me Kalam had more on his mind about people and more likes and dislikes than he let on. He was not as nonchalant about these things as he appeared to be. One day, a woman member of the AIADMK came to see him in the Chennai guest house. Many people would simply come to wish him without appointment, sometimes bearing a gift or a bouquet of flowers. When this person's turn came to go into his room, the staff announced her as being from the 'AIADMK, led by Jayalalithaa'. Perhaps it was a slip of the tongue and his reference was to the guest's name herself, but Kalam asked, within the hearing of not only the woman but also everyone else in the waiting room, 'Who is that?' Now, if you are representing a party and your leader is very popular and you hear this, you are bound to relay it back to your leader. And there were other witnesses too. At that time she was not in power; otherwise she was known, if provoked, to have 'banished' people from the state using very strong language. That must have set the final seal on their relationship and Jayalalithaa snubbed him at every opportunity thereafter.

In 2011 after the state elections of Kerala, West Bengal and Tamil Nadu, Kalam wanted to wish all the newly elected chief ministers. He asked me one morning to connect him to all the newly elected chief ministers. He wished Oommen Chandy in Kerala, who expressed great happiness at Kalam's gesture of congratulating him. Then I connected him to Mamata Banerjee of West Bengal. She spoke to Kalam amid a jubilant crowd of party workers. Mamata Banerjee was always very cordial towards him and received him at Kolkata airport a few times when he visited the state for other functions as former president. Then I tried the Tamil Nadu chief minister, but she never responded. She never came on the phone if our office called hers. Her office continued to tell me that she was busy with MLAs or meeting party workers throughout the day. It was clear that she did not want to talk to him. 'Why aren't you connecting me to her?' Kalam asked me the next day. I told him what was happening and he said, 'Leave it, then.'

Despite the image he tried to project of himself as someone who was indifferent to criticism and unconcerned about petty politics, there were times when his indiscretion could be startling. Sometimes, as the chief guest at a function, he would have to be told who would be sharing the dais with him. He would ask, 'Who is that fellow? And this fellow? That guy?' Often, he was loud enough for the subject to hear, and the subject was invariably a fairly well-known MP or MLA or a prominent political party leader. It was as if he assumed that everybody knew him and that everybody else was less known.

To come back to the AIADMK chief, in 2014, one of Kalam's doctor friends was in need of some land in Chennai for opening an eye hospital. The doctor had got information that such land transactions could not happen without the chief minister's intervention. So he approached Kalam and requested him to introduce him to the chief minister. Since this introduction was for a charitable objective, Kalam wanted to help his friend. He tried once, twice, three times to get in touch with the AIADMK chief, but to no avail. Every time a Poogundrum from her office would tell us that madam was busy and would assure us that the message would be conveyed and the chief minister would call back. But that never happened. Disappointed, Kalam asked us, 'Why can't the chief secretary be contacted if the chief minister is not responding?' So we connected him to the chief secretary. Kalam spoke to the chief secretary and explained the issue to her briefly. She agreed to apprise the chief minister of the matter and revert. But she too never called back. Kalam, predictably, took this in his stride and did not speak about it. Eventually, even at Kalam's funeral, where all the national leaders and chief ministers of the southern states, including the opposition leader from Kerala V.S. Achuthanandan, then ninety years old and in frail health, were present, Jayalalithaa was not to be seen. She sent her ministers, led by her loyal deputy. A clarification was given later that the chief minister could not participate owing to ill health, but that may not have been the entire reason.

In 2012, when it was time for presidential elections again, there seemed to be another sliver of hope that Kalam might get a second term as President when Mamata Banerjee and Mulayam Singh Yadav advanced their list of presidential candidates featuring Kalam at the top. Subramanian Swamy visited Kalam one day to persuade him to contest. Mamata Banerjee and Mulayam were defying the Congress, which had proposed the name of Pranab Mukherjee. Kalam indicated that he was in principle ready to contest, but that he would have to be a consensus candidate and would not proactively take any initiative in the matter. Mamata Banerjee was at the forefront, mounting support for him. She and Mulayam had a substantial number of MPs with them, and their withdrawal from the government would have posed a threat to UPA-II. But Kalam's hopes, if he had any, were dashed when overnight Mulayam changed his stance and supported the Congress's choice.

Mulayam had had a long and strong friendship with Kalam. I believe that Kalam's nomination for the Bharat Ratna resulted chiefly from Mulayam's efforts. When he was defence minister in the United Front government in the late 1990s, he had ordered that all files sent to him were to be in Hindi. This had put Kalam in a spot. But Mulayam had been very generous towards Kalam and had adjusted his requirements so Kalam could communicate with him in English. And as mentioned already, when the Samajwadi Party chief was debating on whether or not to support the UPA government on the nuclear pact with the US, it was Kalam's expert opinion that he had relied on.

On 12 June 2012, a few days before the presidential elections, we got information that 'Netaji' (as Mulayam is popularly known) wanted to talk to the former president around ten that night. I was in the office and was asked to stay back to attend the call. The call came exactly at 10 p.m. Kalam instructed me to stay near the telephone and translate for him what the SP chief was saying in Hindi. What Mulayam said was, 'Hum kal aap ka naam propose karne ja rahe hain. Aap tayyar hain?' Mulayam wanted to know if Kalam was agreeable to his name being announced by the Samajwadi Party and Trinamool Congress as their presidential candidate the next day. Kalam replied, in his style of Hindi, 'Achcha hai ... Ready. OK.' That was the brief conversation they had.

The next day, however, events took a different turn, resulting in big drama. What transpired that night is a mystery. But at a press conference that day Mulayam announced that his party was supporting Pranab Mukherjee for President. Some scribes asked him about his previous support of Kalam. He snapped, 'Who is Kalam? Who told you the name Kalam?' At this point, without uttering a word, Mamata Banerjee walked out of the press conference and went straight to the airport. She understood that she had been ditched by Mulayam. I learnt later that she never spoke to him again after that.

A little while later, Kalam received another message through one of his secretary friends. Apparently, it was a message from someone whose party favoured the other candidate asking Kalam to withdraw. Kalam did not react or respond. He had clearly decided to keep out of the presidential race altogether.

Since the beginning Narendra Modi and Kalam had shared a congenial relationship. Whenever there was an important function in Gujarat, Modi, as the chief minister, used to invite Kalam, and the latter reciprocated favourably. If the invitation was from Modi, a Gujarat trip was assured for Kalam. It was like 'Modi invites, Kalam goes'. The blip in their relationship happened in 2013. Kalam was in Gujarat at the chief minister's invitation to address a government function on 29 June on the theme of good governance. After the function, the two spent time in a room adjacent to the venue. Modi told Kalam that he wanted him to lay the foundation stone for a big statue of Sardar Patel, which was going to be the largest statue in the country. For the first time, Kalam politely declined a request from him saying that as a matter of principle he had stopped laying foundation stones and unveiling statues. The chief minister followed up the invitation with a letter the next day. Once again Kalam declined politely.

It was several months before communications resumed. In March 2014 Kalam received a message about the ailing Brahmaswarup Pramukh Swami Maharaj of the BAPS Swaminarayan sect, whom he respected a lot. The swami stayed in his ashram in Sarangpur village in Botad district of Gujarat, about 150 kilometres from Ahmedabad airport. Since it was a long journey by road, I suggested to Kalam that we request the chief minister's office for a helicopter for the journey to and from Ahmedabad airport to Sarangpur to avoid a tiring road journey. Kalam was dead against making any such request to the government, that too after he had declined the chief minister's request a few months earlier. Still, at my persuasion, Kalam agreed and allowed me to contact the chief minister's office. I texted Sanjay Bhavsar, officer on special duty to the chief minister, and in no time permission was granted through WhatsApp for use of the helicopter.

Despite this, the silence between Kalam and Modi continued. Two months later, the NDA, led by Modi, won a landslide victory in the general elections. Usually, Kalam took the initiative to call the winning candidate. This time there was conspicuous hesitancy on his part. Ultimately, one evening, I had to remind him repeatedly to call the prime-minister-designate to congratulate him. When I prompted him he would say, 'Oh, BJP has won majority? So, he [Modi] is the prime minister?' But he never asked me to connect him to the prime-minister-in-waiting. I continued to remind him about it until he finally agreed to talk to Modi. It was the last week of May and Modi was at Gujarat Bhavan, waiting to take charge. I connected Kalam to Modi through the resident commissioner Gujarat who was with him. They talked for some time. Kalam said, 'Modiji, congratulations. You work for a new India, greater India. Work for Vision 2020. My programme is already there.' From his expression, I figured that there was cordial reciprocation from the other side. Later, Kalam was formally invited to the swearing-in ceremony, which he attended. There can be two reasons for the unusual hesitancy Kalam had exhibited in congratulating Modi: one, his general lethargy and slowness following an illness in November 2013, and two, he did not want any comment that he was trying to get close to the powers that be. Kalam was very proud of a ten-point note he had prepared to give

Modi in anticipation of a meeting after Modi became prime minister, when he was to visit him at Rajaji Marg. Apparently, the visit did not happen.

There is no guarantee that anyone, however good, will be loved by everyone or all the time. I think it is natural that someone or the other will dislike you. Sometimes it is not your fault or failing but circumstances that lead to such a situation. Kalam was extremely sensitive to being disliked, but on the whole, most people considered him a dignified celebrity.

6

A Fresh Start

On 25 July 2007 Kalam demitted office. His last day in office was a very busy one. After breakfast, Kalam was at the Central Hall of Parliament by 11 a.m. The swearing-in ceremony went off smoothly. After that he and President Pratibha Patil returned together to Rashtrapati Bhavan, where the formal handing over happened, followed by lunch. The new President then accompanied Kalam to his temporary guest house accommodation provided by the army and after a formal tea she returned to Rashtrapati Bhavan. That was the protocol.

All the staff working for Kalam were at the army guest house before Kalam arrived. For a brief while, there seemed to be nothing to do. We sat together to plan for the next activities and had tea, but my mind was racing. I was worried about my accommodation. I would soon have to move out of the presidential estate, and no house had been allotted to me though it was all sanctioned on paper. Because of Kalam's packed schedule, his staff never had the time to do their personal work. But the good soul solved my problem for me, and I will come to that later.

Kalam had moved out with two or three trunks of books, a few clothes and some daily-use items. He could not care less. All the personal gifts made to him he donated to the Rashtrapati Bhavan museum.

As former president, Kalam could get a house anywhere in the country. He decided to live in Delhi. Once this decision was taken the urban development ministry came up with suggestions. They showed him two or three houses. If he had had a wife and children, they would probably have helped him choose one. My colleague and I were the family substitutes for Kalam, and we went with him to look at the houses. Kalam had in mind a ground-floor office, a first-floor library and a small room for himself. He was not concerned about the rest of the house and its layout. However, the houses available were mostly single-storey bungalows. Finally, the Estates Department found a suitable bungalow on Rajaji Marg. It was occupied by two senior bureaucrats. They were allotted alternative accommodation and asked to vacate quickly as the bungalow had to be renovated for the former president. With great reluctance and some resistance the two officials vacated the bungalow. It took an unusually long time for the building to be renovated to Kalam's specifications, and for some reason the concerned departments were uncooperative and slow.

We had to muster the support of some of Kalam's old colleagues to get the house transformed to suit his requirements. The first floor was made his residence; it had a big hall, a bedroom and a library. A drawing room and offices were created on the ground floor. Office equipment, including computers, a fax machine and printers, were procured through an NGO because as per government rules these were not allotted to a former president. Most of his predecessors had not asked for any such things since they mostly spent a carefree retired life. But such a lifestyle did not suit Kalam.

Right from day one he planned for his next six months. There was travel involved, with invitations for programmes that had to be accepted. Within a week of the handing over of the house, things were on track. Kalam had been provided security by the Ministry of Home Affairs (MHA). He had also been provided a car and a driver. But our request for an additional car for him as a standby was rejected by the MHA. Kalam did not want to make any special request to the then ruling party. Still, on our request, keeping in view the heavy schedule and coordination work involved with other departments, he wrote a note to the concerned authority but was politely refused by the department quoting rules framed in the 1960s and 1970s.

That silence over tea, when we suddenly found ourselves deposited in the army guest house from Rashtrapati Bhavan, was all too brief. A new surge of enthusiasm seemed to have swept over Kalam once he relinquished office. He became extremely energetic and eager to engage with the public, particularly the youth. It appeared as though he was a fish getting back to its pond. The demands for his presence across the country matched his enthusiasm too. In no time a deluge of requests from various parts of the country, from various organizations – NGOs, educational institutions, state governments – drowned us. Even before we could get a grip on the changed routine, he got us engaged in fixing his hectic programmes and travel schedules. Even at the army guest house, when there was no proper office or staff support, we still managed his demands and fulfilled his wishes. Perhaps he wanted to show the UPA chairperson that he was much more popular than anybody then. But like a great statesman he kept his feelings to himself.

Former presidents are entitled to six staff members for running their office – a private secretary, two additional private secretaries, one personal assistant, a peon and a driver – whom they can select from the government service or from outside. I had been asked to continue with Kalam. So all the heavy work got diverted my way. I was constantly in touch with various agencies to organize his programmes without any hiccups. I was surprised at the number of good souls all over the country who had special respect and affection for Kalam. They corresponded with us with great cordiality and our job gradually got easier. Soon, former president Kalam was again travelling regularly, visiting every nook and corner of the country, where again crowds collected everywhere, even at the state guest houses where he used to stay. The pace of travel was such that he would return to Delhi from a two- or three-day trip and leave early the next morning for another part of the country – something even the airline staff used to comment on. We were at great pains to accommodate the requests of the common people to meet him, and this was the case from Kashmir to Kanyakumari.

People seemed to respond more fervently to Kalam in his new avatar as former president of India. State and local governments at all levels held him in high regard and accorded him a grand welcome wherever he went. The arrangements and reception at state capitals were the same as those accorded to the first citizen. The media seemed eager to cover his events. It was educational institutions that wanted him most for their various anniversaries, centenary celebrations, convocations, and so on. Kalam was the first choice for many of those organizers. I came to know the prime minister, president and ministers were considered only on Kalam's non-availability. Such was his popularity. My table at the office had piles of invitations, and I am not exaggerating when I say that we would present only ten of several requests to Kalam, who would then choose two or three from our shortlist. He made at least ten trips every month. These included visits abroad for a couple of days each to countries such as the US, Indonesia and the Netherlands. All this within five months of demitting office. I could not go home on time, and had little rest. Even on Sundays I was able to enjoy a holiday only after special appeals.

A full programme-packed month had passed and I was in a dire situation. I had not got alternative accommodation and I was still living in the Rashtrapati Bhavan staff quarters with my family. The new private secretary to the president was mounting pressure on me to vacate my accommodation. My days were chock-full of Kalam's work. In Delhi, everything is available within arm's reach but not accommodation. I mustered all the available energy and free time I could and scoured government quarters in nearby areas to find an available flat. Finally with the help of a friend and fellow government servant, I found one that was close to the office and had recently been vacated. Now, to pursue the concerned offices and get the paperwork moving to have it allotted to me was another Herculean task!

I managed to submit a formal request to the housing ministry, only to get a reply saying no houses were currently vacant. I took an appointment to meet the private secretary to the minister for urban development. He, as is always with the IAS, rejected my request for a house close to Kalam's bungalow commenting: 'Kalam is retired now, so what's the great work he has to do that your presence is required at such close quarters?'

Finally, I felt so pressured – with Kalam's work on the one hand and reminders to vacate the house in the presidential estate on the other – that I had no option but to approach Kalam. 'Sir, you have got these back-to-back programmes and travels. But I am facing a grave issue. I have to vacate my current residence and am not getting any accommodation. I have already identified a vacant flat. Please talk to Honourable Minister Jaipal Reddy for help.' That was the only way to get allotment fast.

The very next morning Kalam asked me to connect him to Jaipal Reddy. I did so. He asked me to stand nearby so that I could hear the conversation. Kalam said, 'Jaipal Reddy sir, it's Kalam here. See, one of my guys [he always introduced his staff in this manner] has got a problem getting allotment of house. There is no accommodation allotted to him. But there is a vacant house in [a particular area]. Can you do something to help him?' The minister replied, 'Definitely, sir. We will do that.' Jaipal Reddy then seized the opportunity to invite Kalam to visit the school in his village and address the students on his next visit to Hyderabad. Kalam agreed then and there. After the conversation he said to me, 'To get your work done I have to oblige his request.' Immediately, Reddy's office called for my papers. Kalam had talked to the minister at 10.30 a.m. and by 4 p.m. the allotment letter was in my hand.

With my problem solved in a single day, I was so grateful I threw myself even more fervently into work at Kalam's office. He travelled a lot, and everywhere he went he was treated like a sitting president and the state paraphernalia was rolled out for him. Being a former president, Kalam was provided Z+ category security. There were thirty-two Delhi Police personnel at any time guarding his residence. To Kalam they were merely decorative, I think, and anyone who wished to meet the former president could simply walk into the premises. And if he was present, he would definitely meet them.

Once a visitor came by autorickshaw. The driver of the rickshaw pleaded with me to be allowed to see Kalam, at least from a distance. I went inside and told Kalam that an autorickshaw driver was waiting outside and wished to see him. 'Oh, he wants to see me,' said Kalam, and shot out of the door immediately. He walked to the auto driver, grabbed his hands and said, 'Thank you so much for visiting my house.' The driver was also allowed to take a photograph with him. When the passenger whom the auto driver had brought to Kalam's residence came by, presumably to pay the driver, the driver told him emotionally, 'Sir, I don't need any money. I got to meet the President of India. That is enough.' And he drove away.

Even the police personnel who had provided security for so many VIPs were extra enthusiastic and pleased to be posted at Kalam's home. I love to be at the gates of Kalam sa'ab's house rather than doing station duty, I have been told by a couple of them. They took pride in telling their families that they were providing security for Kalam; they used his name rather than his designation – 'I am posted as Kalam's security' instead of 'former president's security'.

Many others continued addressing or referring to Kalam as 'President' even after he had stopped being one. Sometimes invitation cards too were printed with this mistake and I had to correct many institutions and their event organizers in this regard. They would often reply saying that for them he was still the President of India!

Various authorities and the top brass of state and local governments made tremendous efforts to ensure that the former president's visit became a memorable milestone in the history of their village, town or city. Now that Kalam was no longer president, he was even more accessible to the public. One such visit to a remote village in Wayanad district in Kerala stands out. The reception he received there was a reflection of the immense respect and affection the people of the country had for him.

Kalam was invited by the district collector of Wayanad to launch a project called 'Arividam', an educational web portal for schools in Wayanad. In addition he had to visit the Jawahar Navodaya Vidyalaya at Vythiri, a distant town in the district. I had procured air tickets in such a way that we would depart Delhi by an 11 a.m. flight, reach Bangalore at 1.30 p.m. and then board another flight to Kozhikode so as to reach our destination by 4.30 p.m. From Kozhikode to Wayanad, a distance of 90 kilometres, we would travel by road. But the flight from Delhi got delayed by over three hours due to February fog, throwing the whole plan into disarray. I asked Kalam if we should cancel the Wayanad programme. He said, 'No, no, nothing doing. Don't cancel. Instead, have a word with the district collector of Wayanad to know the exact condition, in case we reach there late.' I got in touch with the district collector, who said no change could be made to the programme, but that they would wait for Kalam, however long it took. I asked him what the people who were waiting for Kalam would do. The collector confidently assured me that a huge crowd had already gathered, and they were prepared to wait any length of time for Kalam. Nothing could be done now – Kalam would simply have to make it.

In Delhi, we decided to board the delayed flight. We reached Bangalore at 5.45 p.m. We had missed the connecting flight to Kozhikode, of course. The only way out was to take the road from Bangalore to Wayanad, which was largely through a forest that is a restricted zone after 6 p.m. We had alerted the authorities in Bangalore about Kalam's visit and they had made arrangements for road travel. The convoy of vehicles and security arrangements were in place when we got there. But now we faced another hurdle. Due to wildlife movement, a stretch of road from Mandya to Kerala remains closed during the night. I contacted the Wayanad district collector and the Mandya collector and requested their help. The Mandya collector, without waiting for any orders from his bosses, contacted the Chief Conservator of Forests in Bangalore, and the district forest administration was directed to keep the road open during the night for the smooth passage of Kalam and his entourage. We reached Mandya by around 8.30 p.m. There the collector had arranged quick refreshments for everyone before we set off. He informed his counterpart in Wayanad that we had left Mandya around 9.30 p.m.

As we proceeded along the ghat road through thick forest land, a convoy of eight to ten vehicles, the security posts all along the way waved us ahead. It was 1 a.m. when we reached Wayanad and made our way to the ground where the programme had been organized. We were astounded to see a crowd of about 2,000, all in a jovial and festive mood. Kalam was overwhelmed, also a bit embarrassed for having kept that crowd (consisting mostly of families) waiting. He wanted me to find out if the crowd had eaten or had gone hungry. The collector told me, 'Don't worry. We have arranged food for you and have provided packets of biryani for everyone gathered here.' I could not contain my surprise, 'Sir, how could you arrange food for this huge gathering at this hour of night!' The district collector replied, 'Since this is Kalam's programme, the hotel owners in the town who are his ardent fans provided the food packets free of cost to the entire crowd gathered at the venue.'

Kalam received a rousing reception from that crowd. Children and women cheered as he appeared. It was a massive welcome. I was unable to contain my emotions, and tears rolled down my face. Kalam, who anyway did not need much by way of motivation to feel energetic and enthusiastic, was galvanized by the crowd. He spoke to them for about one and a half hours, in Malayalam, English and Tamil, and the audience responded with unbridled enthusiasm.

There was one more event on the agenda: meeting students of Navodaya Vidyalaya. When we reached the school, it was 2.30 a.m. The teachers had persuaded their students to take a nap and had woken them up as the former president arrived. None looked any less fresh for having waited overnight, and neither did Kalam, after that long journey and the taxing programmes. His interaction with the students went on for over an hour, when a wholesome breakfast of dosa, idli, chutney, sambar and tea arrived, organized by C.V. Shanti, the dynamic principal of the school.

After the programme, we reached the Kozhikode state guest house at daybreak. We, Kalam's team, slept till 7 a.m. We did not want to wake up Kalam as he had had a very tiring schedule the previous day. Yet, we were aware that if he woke up late, that day's programmes would be thrown out of schedule. And then would come the sequence of juggling travel arrangements, and so on. I was on my toes. It appeared that Kalam had hardly slept. In the morning the lights were on; had he gone to sleep immediately upon occupying the room, he'd have put them out. So we did not have to wake him up, for shortly after we were up Kalam emerged from his room and had tea. By 9 a.m., he was fresh and ready. There was a programme at an orphanage in Mukkam town to meet and address the children and then another programme at a famous women's college in the city. We departed for Delhi late that day.

I wondered how Kalam had so firmly secured a place in the minds and hearts of so many. His security of about 200 policemen on his Kerala trip appeared to be so happy to be there. Across Tamil Nadu and Kerala, women carrying babies would line up along Kalam's route to see him and wave to him. I asked one woman in Kerala why she had brought her baby to the event. 'We want our babies to receive his blessing, sir,' she replied. Kalam once jokingly mentioned to me that perhaps he should stand for elections from one of these places. In Kerala he was particularly popular and was the first choice of chief guest for any important event. As we have seen, when he addressed the legislature in Kerala, every MLA turned up, whether from the ruling party or the opposition.

Many state governments continued to invite him for various functions. The chief minister of Gujarat invited Kalam in December 2009 to address his officers at a chintanshivir organized in Kutch. There was hardly a week when Kalam did not visit one state or another. Be it an event at a primary health centre or a postgraduate medical institute, an orphanage or a large spiritual centre, Kalam was in high demand everywhere. Everyone wanted Kalam's presence to grace their milestone occasions. It was impossible for Kalam to oblige everyone, so we would gather as much information as we could about the institute in question and decide whether Kalam ought to accept the invitation or not. Once something was finalized, we would sit together and accommodate a few other programmes in the vicinity to utilize the trip to the maximum. Acceptance of invitations was after a thorough verification of the background and antecedents of the organizers through the district administration. We had to sometimes reject or cancel a few invitations at the last minute after receiving an adverse report from the local administration.

One only needs to consider Kalam's first few months after demitting office to get a sense of his frenzied energy. Kalam left Rashtrapati Bhavan on 25 July. On 26 July, he was at Anna University in Chennai to interact with the students. The next day too was jam-packed. There was no breathing space. My colleague and I decided to take turns to travel with him. I would accompany Kalam on his trips down south and my colleague would travel with him to north India. A month after demitting office, in August–September, he visited the US on invitation from a university, and that programme required much preparation. September was filled with visits abroad. I accompanied him to Indonesia and to the Netherlands a month later. He mostly addressed the Indian communities there, who attended in large numbers. As always, he took the trouble to make his speeches there interesting with relevant facts, insights and suggestions. In October there was another US visit and November was filled with domestic visits. Those were his first few months of freedom from presidency!

In 2008, when he visited Kentucky, the Gatton College of Business and Economics, University of Kentucky, Lexington, invited him to be distinguished visiting professor and stay with them for a month in a year. He was to give lectures to postgraduate and PhD students. It was an honorary role, but his stay and travel would be taken care of. He readily accepted it, and agreed to visit them again soon.

As part of the presidential entourage I travelled abroad with President Kalam to fifteen countries, namely Russia, the UAE, Bulgaria, Sudan, Switzerland, South Korea, Myanmar, Mauritius, Singapore, South Africa, Iceland, Ukraine, the Philippines, Greece and France. Even when he was no longer president, Kalam was equally popular abroad and invitations were plenty. As former president's aide I travelled with him to many countries, including the US, Canada, the Netherlands, Indonesia, Singapore, Malaysia, Muscat, the UAE, Bangladesh and Bahrain.

During such visits, Kalam unhesitatingly introduced his team members to heads of nations. That was a rare gesture and his large-heartedness was especially remarkable in an environment where leaders projected only themselves and people working for them were all in the shadows and behind the curtain.

I often felt it was all too much for me. I did not have the energy to cope with this punishing schedule. But I had no choice, I was bound to him. One option for me was to return to the defence department. But that meant I would go to some unknown office and sit in some remote corner. Having come from working with an illustrious personality, I would be humiliated by the people around – that is how the junior government ecosystem is. I consulted some of my department people too. Their advice was, 'If he wants you, continue to work with him.' According to the rules, after your deputation, you have to come back to your parent department. And it is difficult to ignore your colleagues. They will keep the jibes and comments going till they fall down exhausted, till they feel they have broken you. I wanted to avoid this 'teasing', which is actually harassment.

I thought to myself, let things go the way they are. There would be no change in level or pay, so why go back? Also, Kalam seemed to have a mission in life, and his enthusiasm was infectious. There was nothing really to worry about other than travel, travel and more travel, which no other former president had ever undertaken. In fact, it was as though he wanted to forget that he was no longer president. So I continued with Kalam, sorting out the invitations piled up on my table. And travelling with him to cities, towns and sometimes deep into villages.

Small colleges in small towns and villages would invite him to visit them and address the students. Once other institutions in the area got wind of it, they would ask for his presence too, so a chain of functions would result. Even the media began to comment on how Kalam had more programmes and invitations than the sitting president.

I wondered what made him so charismatic. Maybe it was his rectitude, his extolling of democratic values and his constant concern about what he felt were two major social evils: corruption and religious fanaticism. People must have sensed that here was a person who had no hidden agenda.

Airline crew too would be excited to have him on board, even after he was no longer president. He was allowed to be driven up to the plane at most major domestic airports and was perhaps the only leader to often have the entire crew led by the captain coming to his seat and wishing him before take-off. Air India, IndiGo, Jet, SpiceJet – all held him in great regard and would announce his presence on board.

Once, Kalam could not have his meal before leaving his official residence to catch a flight. And for medical reasons, he needed to eat at designated hours. But he was travelling by JetLite, which served no food on board. So, before leaving for the airport, I contacted the manager of the airline and requested him to provide food for our party of three, including Kalam. I assured him we would pay for the food. Without a moment's hesitation, he agreed to make the necessary arrangements. The flight took off, and in a while the crew came to us with three packets of food. As we began to eat, we heard a slight commotion behind us. The crew were distributing food packets to all the passengers, but they were refusing them as they feared they would be charged for it. We could hear the crew explaining to them that no payment was required and that it was complimentary, for the former president was on the flight! I had asked for just three packets of food against payment, but the airline served food for all the passengers free of cost, in honour of Kalam.

People ask me whether Kalam had any hobbies. I have already written about his great love for Carnatic music. He had several CDs, which he used to play often. Another great liking of his was shehnai, particularly that of Ustad Bismillah Khan, which was his favourite music for mornings. It was played at a low volume in his bedroom. He had a limited number of music CDs, mostly of flute, violin and shehnai music, and he would play them over and over. As

President, he had even hosted several music concerts at Rashtrapati Bhavan.

As for sports, he used to tell us that he had played badminton in his college days. And he was interested in cricket in a strange way. He never watched matches, but had the radio on for updates. If he was busy and could not have the radio on, anyone who entered the room would be asked for the latest score. He never watched television. Even when there was breaking news, he only read the papers or followed the radio.

During his free time, he would read books, and in due course he was writing them too. Books were the only gifts he accepted; other costly gifts he either refused or returned politely. Practically every piece of furniture in his house, including the chairs, was loaded with books, and he had to often clear a space for himself to sit and do some work. There were papers, books and reports everywhere, and, as at Rashtrapati Bhavan, every time one of these was needed we would have to ferret out the right document for him. There would be reports several years old lying about.

Anybody who entered his room would be struck by how small the man of the house looked in the midst of these giant piles of papers and books. They'd be led to believe much hard work was happening there. Actually, whatever report came he would ask us to make three copies of it and keep the original with him. His idea was that if the original was lost there would be three copies left still. Only when he went overseas did we get an opportunity to clear the mess, because when he was around he would be very annoyed to see us touching his books and papers, whereas even if he complained after returning, nothing could be done. We did this for years, right from his days at the defence ministry. 'OK, where is that report, have you destroyed it?' he would ask. We would simply blink, and that was it. We would remove only old reports, additional copies or books he no longer needed. So there was no cause for complaint. He did appreciate a clean table and room!

Even as President, his round dining table, where tea and snacks were served, had to be cleared every day and the books put back in the library. He would always accuse us of throwing away this or that book. He had told the attendants at Rashtrapati Bhavan to keep away from his books. Attendants have always complained to me about there being no space on the table to place his lunch or tea. Find space somewhere else, he would tell them.

Mornings would be spent with his books, either in reading or writing, or in preparation for his speeches. Every day, some fifteen to twenty people would meet him. Sometimes there would be larger crowds. Someone with an invitation to their daughter's wedding, someone with the entire family in tow. The meetings would go on till 10.30 p.m. Some would spend ten minutes with him, some half an hour. They could be teachers, retired people, company officials. Kalam enjoyed these meetings. Until 10.30 p.m, there was no time for him to feel bored or lonely, if he did feel that way at all. After that he would busy himself with reading and his winding-down routine.

He had a dedicated clothesmaker, and my colleague or I would remind him to make fresh bandgalas or shirts for Kalam when the current wardrobe began to look worn out or faded. The clothesmaker had his measurements and would just come and hand over his clothes. His shoes were a particular design of Bata in black known as No. 7. He wore only white or blue shirts and black trousers. When retiring for the night he would wear a dhoti and a shirt. He only wore white dhotis, not lungis.

After demitting the office of President, he had four jawans deputed to him – Havildar V. Chellappa, one cook, M. Diwakar, and two attendants, Christu Das and Kantha Sekhar – as a goodwill gesture by the Indian Army. They were young, maybe in their early thirties. They were incredibly efficient and dedicated to Kalam, and very happy and proud to be working for him. They would say that even their generals had not been so close to a president. They claimed that people from their units, even brigadiers and colonels, would call them to say, 'Do minute dilao saab ke saath photo kheenchne ke liye.' And when they went back to their units, they were treated like VIPs.

Kalam was lucky in the matter of his cook. You had to eat his food to appreciate his talent – dosa, idli, uttappam, they would turn out just right. And he would put so much effort into it. He himself would visit the grocers to pick the best rice and urad for the idlis and the best arhar dal and vegetables for the sambar. The other staff who went with the cook to the market would be frustrated with the time he took for shopping. He would spend more than three hours at a single shop.

Kalam had not been a man particularly bothered about food, he only wanted something provided at the right time. But with this cook, he began to appreciate food quite a bit. When he had friends over he'd say, 'Ask him to prepare some Andhra/Karnataka items. Ask him to serve that Andhra achar.'

The cook and attendants who served him food and took care of his clothes never had to be told what to do. Tea at 6 a.m., breakfast at 10.30 a.m., then lunch, tea again and dinner at the appointed times, all served piping hot. Kalam enjoyed the genius of this cook and the dedication of his attendants right up to the end of his life in July 2015.

Looking back, I feel certain that I would have got bored working in any other department. From 2007 to 2015, I got to know so many people from so many institutions. Until then I had been in a bigger office at Rashtrapati Bhavan, but I had had no direct contact with anyone, as there was another wing taking care of programmes. Here, I got to know many prominent people from up close.

Kalam was liked by many but was selective in forming friendships. Not everyone who tried to get into his orbit made it. He avoided people of disrepute – those with a history blemished by corruption – not only because he did not approve of them but also because he was careful to preserve his reputation.

Major General (Retd) Swaminathan, his long-time intimate colleague, friend and philosopher, was the one he depended on for discussions on any trivial issues. While Kalam was head of a DRDO lab in Hyderabad, Swaminathan had been the person in charge of its management services. He was brought to Delhi as Chief Controller of Resources when Kalam became DRDO chief. A year after Kalam became President, he got Swaminathan inducted to help him and advise him on his various presentations and speeches.

When they had some time, they used to talk about everything under the sun. Swaminathan was an electrical engineer, and something of a versatile genius. He would be at the Technology Interface (TI) room established by Kalam at Rashtrapati Bhavan for discussion and preparation of his speeches/lectures and presentations. It was at the TI room that the speeches were projected on a screen for Kalam and Swaminathan to sit, discuss and edit. Sometimes, we too were asked to join the process. I used to be highly amused to hear them seriously discussing a topic and then seamlessly slip into discussing trivial stuff. There would be long-winded discussions on dosa, idli, rasam and pickle. Swaminathan would say something was best had with buttermilk. And Kalam would say, yes, but with some pickle to go with it.

After demitting office, Kalam asked Swaminathan to join him and he was accommodated in a modified residential facility in the premises of Kalam's Rajaji Marg house. Swaminathan would research the topic of Kalam's presentations and speeches and prepare an impressive speech and keep tweaking it to Kalam's satisfaction. Later, he had to use a walking stick to get about, but he was still a regular at Kalam's office in Rajaji Marg. He worked for Kalam all hours of the day, all days of the week until the sudden decline of his health and unexpected death in 2013. Kalam was crushed. He had lost a good, resourceful person who had had no personal expectations. He never asked for any honour or award from Kalam, unlike many others who surrounded him only for their personal benefit, hoping he could be persuaded to recommend them for a Padma award or government posting. One of Kalam's last books was dedicated to him.

Kalam would be approached by several of his old friends for some favour or the other. Some would seek his support for nomination for national awards or recognitions. Kalam usually did not recommend anybody for any such awards or recognitions but there were exceptions. In his final years he became more liberal and that earlier rigidity faded. And many got favours like nominations for Padma awards, nomination to institutions, etc. However, after 2014 none of his nominations were accepted or considered by the new government.

Kalam had very few friends with whom he could discuss anything personal. The topic of conversation was always events happening in the country, how to improve education, or some such thing. Some connections of his went back forty years. There were some colleagues from his ISRO and DRDO days with whom he remained in touch. A few used Kalam's name to extract favours from organizations and business houses without his knowledge.

I observed right from the Ministry of Defence days that Kalam never entertained women visitors. If any were visiting for an official purpose, he would always ensure that one of us assistants was in the room, doing some odd job in a corner. I think he feared controversy of any kind.

After Swaminathan's passing, it became difficult for Kalam to prepare his speeches and presentations for his many programmes. The vacuum was filled by V. Ponraj, a resourceful person from the DRDO who had served Kalam brilliantly since his presidency. He was a computer scientist and helped Kalam prepare the technical speeches for his visits to engineering colleges, National Institutes of Technology (NITs) and IITs. He had political ambitions. He co-authored Kalam's aspirational *A Manifesto for Change*. However, the association did not last long.

In 2009, Srijan Pal Singh had joined his office as an intern. He was an engineering graduate and had done his management studies at the Indian Institute of Management Ahmedabad. Kalam helped him get a job on a contract basis so that the young man would get a monthly stipend. The association broke up after some time as Kalam was unhappy with some aspects of his functioning, but after the demise of Major General Swaminathan he was without an assistant for meaningful discussions or to work on his speeches and on the books he was writing. Thus he re-entered the office and was with Kalam till the end.

As for Kalam's family, except for his brother and his niece's sons no one visited him at his Rajaji Marg home.

I last saw them at Rashtrapati Bhavan when he invited the entire family over in the last year of his tenure. They stayed with him for two days. All expenses for the trip, including for their food at Rashtrapati Bhavan, were covered by Kalam. He paid rent for the rooms they occupied. He did not want any talk of his family staying with him at the expense of the government. After his presidency, he was in touch with his family, especially his brother and his niece, daily. His older brother would come every year and spend three or four days with him. Kalam was happy when the family visited his Delhi home and spent time with him during his last few years and would often reschedule all other engagements when they visited. The last time they visited him was in 2014.

When they were in Rajaji Marg, Kalam would specifically instruct the cook to prepare all the dishes they demanded. Most of the time it was a treat of non-vegetarian items. He would adjust his irregular schedule to suit the family. They would often sit together in one room and discuss family issues from their past and catch up on news about marriages and other such events. Kalam visited his home town of Rameswaram only on specific occasions such as the weddings of his grandnieces and grandnephews.

In the late 1990s a telegram arrived at the Army Headquarters communication desk addressed to 'Abdul

Kalam, DRDO, New Delhi'. His family was not aware of the importance of his position as chief of DRDO. At that time, no one in Army Headquarters was familiar with his name or position. The telegram meant for Kalam did the rounds with people trying to locate Kalam, whoever he was. The communication section somehow found out the telephone number of Dr Kalam and called our office. The message was 'BROTHER PASSED AWAY, START IMMEDIATELY' in the usual old-style telegraphic language. I was in the office and I received the message. I did not know how to convey the sad news when I was not even aware that he had a brother.

I tried to locate Kalam, who was at that time somewhere in Kolar, Karnataka, in connection with a trial of some facility of the DRDO. I communicated the message to the concerned director who was hosting him. He in turn told Kalam, reaching him through the defence communication network. After a few hours I got a call from Kalam. He had by then contacted Rameswaram and talked with his elder brother. Kalam spoke to me without any visible emotion: 'The message you got was correct. Something funny has happened at my place. I am going there. Now, you connect me through conference call [our telephone was equipped with that facility at that time] to [two officers]. They have to attend the meetings and deal with the papers which require my immediate attention.' I promptly connected him with the people concerned and they agreed to take care of the official meetings till he returned to headquarters.

Kalam remained incredibly energetic until November 2013, when he had a fall in his bedroom and suffered a mild stroke. I will dwell on the matter of his health, and of my role as his chief caretaker, in the next chapter.

7

A Religious Side

Kalam was not against spirituality or religion, but he did not care for religious or spiritual interactions. He preferred to accept invitations for events of social, educational or scientific significance. And even there, he preferred events where he could address school or college students. However, as a former president it was not possible for him to avoid them altogether, and he did visit a number of religious destinations and meet with high-profile spiritual and religious leaders.

As I have mentioned earlier, he had told us that he offered namaz every day, but it astounds me that over two decades of fairly intimate association with him, I never saw him perform namaz even once. He must have prayed in his room, no doubt. But that he was so discreet about it – perhaps because he did not consider it appropriate in view of the government positions he held – I find truly remarkable. After some years with him, I began to notice that he carried a rosary in his pocket. And 2012 onward, there was always a miniature

Koran or prayer book to be packed with his other stuff wherever he went. (We did all the packing for him.) This booklet had not been there earlier. I assumed it was a Koran, as the script looked Urdu or Arabic to me. Kalam could not have read it, as he could not read a single word in Hindi, let alone Urdu. But it was of significance to him, and I think it was gifted to him by his brother.

Inwardly, he must have lived the life of a Muslim, but he never encouraged people from his own community to make claims on him in his personal or official life. I was surprised and also disenchanted to see his lukewarm attitude towards visitors from his community, never mind whether they were ordinary people or elites.

He seemed more hospitable and warm while receiving representatives of other religions. He would spend some time with them, never showing any hurry to end the meeting. He must have thought that he did not need to prove his devotion to anyone or strongly identify with his faith. If one is faithful to one's beliefs there is no need for undue expression of them. Your faith is already there in your blood, in your thoughts and way of life. Your faith is your intimate private possession. What was necessary was acceptance of and respect for other faiths. This is my understanding of his religious life, both from observing him and from his stray comments on the subject.

In 1999, while Kalam was with the DRDO, he wished to visit the Kanchi Kamakoti Peetham. As he wanted to keep his visit under wraps, all the arrangements had to be made at the last hour. He needed a dhoti, since he did not have a good one, and a shirt in his favourite sky-blue colour to wear for the meeting with the Shankaracharya. I had to procure them from a Co-optex showroom in Delhi. I bought two dhotis – one with a light-blue border, the other with a maroon one. I also arranged for his travel to Chennai and from there to the Kanchi Kamakoti Peetham. I did not sense any great eagerness in him to make the visit, and perhaps the wish came from his desire to accommodate different faiths. I could only speculate, as he would never tell me why he wanted to make the visit. That visit was in the news for the manner in which Kalam, a famous scientist, received the Shankaracharya's blessings seated below him. After visits to holy places or seers, he would sometimes describe to us the spiritual experience he had. And in his speeches, maybe mention one or two things the person he had met had said that he considered worthy of passing on.

I have mentioned the wristwatch he got from Sai Baba of Puttaparthi, which the latter had produced from thin air and gifted him. This too happened on a visit while he was at the DRDO. One afternoon Kalam called me to his room and said, 'I have to meet Sathya

Sai Baba. Some message has come to me.' He did not disclose what the message was, or whom it had come from. 'I will go to Bangalore. From there you arrange for my travel to Puttaparthi,' he told me. He returned to Delhi after two days and showed me a watch. He was rather curious about this watch that had been produced from thin air. He wanted me to take it to a watch shop to get the length of its gold strap adjusted to fit his wrist. In the evening, on my way home, I took the gift to a watch shop. On seeing it, the man at the shop exclaimed in excitement, 'Oh saab! From where did you get this? This is a very costly watch and is worth nearly one lakh rupees.' The watch 'magically produced' by Sai Baba cost one lakh, I thought to myself. I told the man, 'This watch belongs to a rich man who got it as a gift. Don't ask me anything more about it, you simply adjust the strap and give it back.' When I returned the watch to Kalam the next day, I told him it was a luxury item valued at one lakh rupees. He responded with his usual 'Oh, I see!'

Kalam had been so frugal all his life in everything he did that he was quite alarmed to have something as costly as this. I knew that even six hundred rupees was an exorbitant amount for him, as whenever he needed to buy something he would assign the shopping either to me or to my colleague and was always surprised at how expensive things were. So he kept the costly new watch aside and started using the old one with the leather strap again. I asked him why. 'See, it is a very costly watch and I'll attract criticism for using luxury products,' he replied. But a fortnight later, I saw Kalam wearing the costly watch. He told me that someone had reported to Sai Baba that he was not wearing the watch and that the godman had sent a message to Kalam to use it.

As a native of Kerala, I was his source of information regarding anything related to that state. Occasionally a religious or spiritual institution would get incorporated into Kalam's Kerala visits. Santhigiri Ashram was one of them. The ashram is in Pothencode, a village in Thiruvananthapuram district, established by Navajyothisree Karunakara Guru and currently led by his principal disciples. It is considered an abode of peace and spirituality.

While scheduling a presidential visit to Kerala in 2006, I received a communication from the ashram chief requesting a visit by the President to the ashram. I asked Gururetnam Jnana Thapaswi, the chief priest, to send a formal invitation. I placed it before the President, who keenly listened to me describe Santhigiri Ashram and its social missions under the leadership of Navajyothisree Karunakara Guru's chosen disciple, Sishyapoojitha Amritha Jnana Thapaswini. The invitation was then shared with the secretary to the

President and his military secretary for consideration. Both were not in favour of the visit following the advice they received from the Kerala government. The state's DGP told Kalam's military secretary that the distance involved (90 kilometres from the city), the timing of the visit, the village itself and the road that led to it, which was poorly lit, would present a range of security issues. Hence they did not recommend it be included in the schedule.

I was keen that the President visit the ashram and again briefed him about the spiritual and social services rendered by it. Kalam was impressed, especially to hear about the Ayurveda and Siddha services at the ashram. He decided he would visit it, but could reach there only at 8.45 p.m. The administration could only advise but not easily refuse the first citizen of the country. The state and district administration were on their toes. Preparations were undertaken on a war footing all the way from Thiruvananthapuram to Pothencode. The road leading to the village was well lit with temporary tube lights all through. President Kalam visited the ashram and had a brief interaction with the to-be successor of the guru, Sishyapoojitha Janani Amritha Jnana Thapaswini. They talked, assisted by translators. On our return I could sense that Kalam was deeply moved by the visit. It had been a place of such intense quiet and peace.

Similarly, in April 2014, Kalam accepted an invitation to visit the Manipal group of institutions in Mangalore and the Yenepoya University, Mangalore. Kalam had lively interactions with the youth at the Manipal Institute of Management and the Yenepoya University. We were about to return to the government circuit house for lunch after the programme when I got a call from the head priest of the famous Udupi Sri Krishna Temple, where the deity is viewed through a nine-holed window. Swamiji said, 'Since Kalam is in our town, why don't you bring him to the temple?' I wondered if it would pose a problem as Kalam was a Muslim. Swamiji brushed away my apprehensions. 'For us Kalam is above religion. I will ensure nothing happens and that no one raises any issue.' I conveyed the message to Kalam, who readily agreed to the visit. I called up Swamiji to tell him the former president would visit, but that it should be a low-profile event. Swamiji sounded jubilant. Nobody other than Kalam's security personnel knew about the visit. Even the district administration did not know! We visited the temple at 2.30 p.m. Swamiji and the priests there received Kalam with a poorna kumbha and led him for darshan of Lord Krishna through the nine-holed window called Navagraha Kitiki. Kalam viewed the deity from a window. 'Oh, this is the famous Krishna,' he said. After that he sat with Swamiji and they talked for a good twenty-five minutes with the help of an interpreter about spirituality and science. Their discussion was mostly about how religions could coexist. Kalam was also honoured with an angavastra. The priests appeared to be his admirers. I felt it was a historic occasion for a non-Hindu statesman with secular leanings to visit such a revered temple. The media did not get wind of it and it was not reported in the press. Only a few local Kannada papers reported it. And thank goodness for that – Kalam would have been mobbed by the media had they been tipped off.

Earlier, in September 2010, Kalam had received an invitation from the bishop at the famous St George Forane Church of Edathua to inaugurate the 200th-year celebrations of the church in Alleppey district, Kerala. Built in 1810, the church has a fascinating history. Kalam was initially not interested, but I felt it was my foremost duty to brief him about its importance as a pilgrimage centre for the Christians of Kerala, and what it would mean for the local population to have him in their village. He agreed to the visit being included in his next Kerala programme. Coincidentally, the church event was slated for 15 October, which was Kalam's birthday. The priests of the church arranged a big birthday reception for Kalam at the venue and it was celebrated in front of hundreds of devotees. In his speech at the church, Kalam talked about how his eightieth orbit around the sun was beginning in a historical church. The people of Edathua were overcome with excitement to have him. On my part I felt proud and blessed that it was my 'divine' destiny to ensure such a great personality's presence at the bicentennial of a sacred place.

His visit to Sivagiri Ashram at Varkala in Thiruvananthapuram district, another historical place and important pilgrimage centre, was also at my initiative. I got Swamiji to invite Kalam for the seventy-eighth anniversary of the annual Sivagiri pilgrimage. Kalam was not aware of its significance, and I briefed him about Sree Narayana Guru, the spiritual and social reformer of Kerala whose order of swamis and sanyasins runs the ashram, and about the secular and humanitarian ideas that the event stood for. Sivagiri houses the reformer's tomb and it also has a temple devoted to Sharada Devi, the goddess of knowledge. Kalam was not familiar with Narayana Guru and was quite keen to learn more about the place. He not only attended the event but visited Sivagiri Ashram that day.

As I have said before, Kalam wanted his religious beliefs to be his exclusively personal matter. Though a faithful follower of his religion, he paid extra care not to exhibit his faith before anyone, particularly in front of his own community. It was more difficult to get him to accept invitations from Muslim organizations. And he was particularly hesitant to visit madrasas.

In December 2010, the chief of the Jamia Markaz in Mukkam, Janab Aboobaker Musaliar, approached him with an invitation. Thinking the markaz was a madrasa, Kalam declined the invitation. He agreed to attend only when I convinced him that the Jamia Markaz was only a yatimkhana and that the audience would be students from various regular educational institutions and not from any madrasa. Kalam's visit to the markaz became a matter of jubilation for Mukkam village, particularly for the Muslim community there.

Ayurveda does not have anything to do with religion, but since it is considered a sacred practice, I should mention Kalam's visit to the Vaidyaratnam Ayurveda facility in Kerala. It is a world-famous Ayurveda centre in Thaikkattussery, Thrissur district. The invitation came from the chief physician, and he wanted Kalam to inaugurate an Ayurvedic museum in the memory of the founder, Vaidyaratnam Ashtavaidyan E.T. Neelakandan Mooss, on his birth centenary. Kalam was only familiar with the name of Kottakkal Arya Vaidya Sala in Kerala. Though he never went for any Ayurvedic treatment himself, he had great respect for the age-old system of medical treatment. Not being familiar with the name of Vaidyaratnam, he put the invitation away somewhere. Since I believed in Ayurveda, I gave Kalam a compelling description of how Neelakandan Mooss had founded this institute in 1941 and how it had expanded since.

Kalam was an open-minded and unprejudiced man, and he heard everything I had to say. He agreed to visit the facility. He gave a stimulating speech at the event and spent forty minutes there after inaugurating the museum.

Strictly speaking, I should not discuss the invitation Kalam received from the Rashtriya Swayamsevak Sangh (RSS) in the same breath as I do the invitations from actual religious institutions, but he once nearly made a trip to their headquarters in Nagpur for a key event with its leaders. In May 2014, our office received an invitation from the secretary general of Vijnana Bharati and the RSS national general secretary, Ram Madhav. They wanted the former president to address young RSS volunteers at a training camp in the presence of the RSS chief Mohan Bhagwat. The camp would conclude on 12 June, and they wished to have Kalam visit before that on a date convenient to him. Ram Madhav later visited Kalam, and it was decided that Kalam would attend the programme at the RSS headquarters on the concluding day of the training camp. In the meantime, as a result of inputs and advice he received from some of his friends, Kalam changed his mind. He was warned by them that a visit to the RSS headquarters would get him labelled as an RSS sympathizer and lead to possible misuse of his name by the organization. Kalam wanted me to provide an excuse to the organization and to say that he would be glad to pay a visit there five days prior to the said event. I really had a tough time talking with the contact person at the RSS. The leadership got really annoyed at this sudden backing out because they had made arrangements and planned for publicity around his visit. A month after the date that he had agreed on, Kalam did visit the RSS headquarters and addressed the participants at an in-house training. Notably, none of the top brass of the organization turned up.

I have said earlier it was Kalam's habit to recollect and reproduce in his speeches some of the virtuous messages he picked up from the spiritual leaders he met. After coming back from Puttaparthi, he often quoted Sai Baba's 'When there is righteousness in the heart, there is beauty in the character. When there is beauty in the character, there is harmony in the home. When there is harmony in the home, there is order in the nation. When there is order in the nation, there is peace in the world.' For several years and at several meetings he used to recite these lines. Though he never claimed they were his own, they became so associated with him that they sometimes pop up in reports or conversations as his own. An Internet search of the lines shows the words being attributed variously to Kalam, to Sai Baba, to Confucius and even rendered as a Scottish saying.

8

Failing Health

Kalam was not interested in his appearance, that is, whether or not he looked good or impressive, and was not particular about his clothes or other accessories. The only exception was his hair. He took a full hour over it, oiling it and combing it this way and that so that it was set to his exact satisfaction. Though he cared little about his looks, he was very different when it came to his health. I don't mean he took care of his health. In fact, he had the most cavalier attitude towards it – his meal timings were random, he did not eat a variety of nutritious foods, he did not allow himself any true leisure time and he travelled too much. But he was inordinately bothered about what others thought of his health. He was seized with fear whenever he thought people might get to know about some physical illness or weakness he might have. It was an obsessive fear. From 1993 to 2002 he had no major health problems except for his perennial tooth issue for which he used to frequent the dental clinic of the DRDO. To prevent any inconvenience to the other staff and scientists of the institute, he would go to the clinic from his office in South Block at 8.45 p.m. and spend three to four hours there with the dental surgeon.

In 2004, he had a fall. During his presidency, it was his morning routine to take two or three rounds of the Mughal Gardens at a leisurely pace. One morning Kalam tried to hop over a row of flowerpots. He considered himself very agile, and he simply jumped from one path to another over a line of flowerpots separating the two. There was some water spilt on the second path, and he slipped and fell. He got up by himself but seemed to have dislocated his shoulder. He returned to his room in great pain, and the Rashtrapati Bhavan doctor had to be called. The doctor recommended that Kalam be taken to hospital: he was the President of the country, and one could not take any chances. He set Kalam's shoulder temporarily with a bandage and gave him painkillers. An ambulance was called and Kalam was taken to hospital.

A team of army doctors discussed the line of treatment. One suggested surgery to set his shoulder in place. Kalam would have none of it. Could surgery not be avoided, he wanted to know. The army doctors said it was not possible. Kalam insisted he wanted to consult an orthopaedist friend in Hyderabad, Dr B.N. Prasad. Dr Prasad was briefed and requested to fly to

Delhi immediately. Arriving in Delhi by evening, he examined Kalam, ruled out surgery and was confident of setting the shoulder right manually. And under local anaesthesia, Kalam's shoulder was manoeuvred into place.

In the battery of tests conducted on Kalam at the hospital, it showed up that he was diabetic and needed medication and diet control. But no warnings could bring about a change to his routine and he continued to take all sorts of food and at his own sweet time, like breakfast at 12.30 p.m., lunch at 4 p.m. or 5 p.m., dinner at 12.30 a.m. or 1 a.m. Dr Prasad said that the President, at seventy-plus years, would have to give his shoulder some time to heal. His arm would have to be in a sling for a month, and he could not travel. Any jerks, such as might happen on a helicopter ride, would delay the healing. Kalam could only attend events in the city.

What Kalam feared happened and the news spread in the media about his indisposition. The events outside Delhi were cancelled and he was confined to the capital. He found it difficult to get on with his daily routine, but continued to attend all important programmes in Delhi with one arm in a sling. Even with this he continued to participate in several important functions at Vigyan Bhavan and received visiting foreign dignitaries on the lawns of Rashtrapati Bhavan. After a month, when the sling was removed, he was all praise for the attendant who had assisted him throughout. 'This guy is a fantastic person, he helped me all through with my daily routines,' he said.

A string of programmes had had to be cancelled. For Kalam this was a nightmare. He feared his reputation would be tainted. So many people must have made so many arrangements; a lot of money would be going down the drain, he complained. Till the end, that was his fear – even when he set off on his Shillong trip, where he collapsed and later died. He was afraid that people would think he was unwell. On the morning of that fateful day, he was feeling uneasy and was not his usual self, as per the attendants, but he kept that to himself. He did not display any uneasiness or discomfort. But doctors later mentioned to me that there must have been discomfort or variations in blood pressure from the day before, which he had ignored or kept secret. He could have cancelled the trip – after all, it was just a lecture – but to keep his word and not disappoint the students waiting for him, he risked his safety and health.

There were early indications of his dislike of being seen as unfit. He would never open the door to his room until he had his dentures on. Naturally, his face would look different with his dentures off, but even after twenty years of knowing us, he would not have us see him toothless even for a second – like the film star and chief minister MGR, whom no one was permitted to see without his fur cap and dark glasses. Only an attendant was allowed in when he was in that state.

During Kalam's presidency too, he could not imagine cancelling programmes. If he was down with a fever or unwell in some way and a programme or two had to be cancelled, he would do it with great reluctance and would dictate to us what to tell the organizers. We could not say the President had had a fall or that he was indisposed. It would have to be a vague statement: 'The President has some difficulties travelling, so his programme has to be rescheduled.'

Here is another glimpse of his stubbornness with respect to his health. In 2008, he had accepted an invitation from the NIT in Dharamshala. The Dalai Lama came to know about it and called us. He wanted Kalam to visit him at his ashram. They spoke for an hour and forty-five minutes. It was early January and the night stay at the NIT campus was not very comfortable. We had not asked for the state government guest house. It was very cold by the time we boarded our flight to Delhi, by which time Kalam was running a slight fever. He did not tell me that he was feeling unwell, though I was sitting next to him on the plane, but by the time we landed he was so unwell that we had to head directly to the Army Hospital, where he stayed for three or four days till his fever subsided. The doctors had to coax him to stay that long. And unwilling to slow down, he began to travel again the very next week.

I think that was his greatest undoing. He might have lived longer had he not pushed himself so much, fearing that people would think he was unwell and unfit. It was not just that he travelled so much, but that his involvement was intense, his preparation was intense. To give you an idea of his preparation, whenever he addressed a group, academic or professional, he would often ask them to repeat a 10-point oath he had designed specially for the occasion. At an educational institution, he would ask the students to take an oath, which might say 'I will love my parents. I will make my mother happy.' The parents in the audience would be overcome by this unique way of interacting with the crowd. After all, who bothered to acknowledge mothers. Once his oath for a group of nurses moved them to tears. Then there were oaths he framed for medical students, engineering students and so on. He liked to tug at their heartstrings in some way.

Not that every speech of his was a hit, but somehow he would make his way into his audience's hearts. Often, his speeches in north India were not even translated accurately. The interpreter would sometimes veer off on a tangent. But no one cared. The audience, especially in small towns and rural areas, would simply mob him afterwards. He had a compelling energy about him and he projected that kind of emotional appeal. Crowds for Kalam were largest in south India and the North-East. At a Coimbatore guest house people once waited for Kalam till one o'clock in the morning, many of them women carrying babies in their arms. He used to wonder why people would wait in the rain, in the pitch-dark, all along the airport road to see him. 'Why are they standing here? Just to see me?' he once asked me. He would then put the lights on in his car and wave to them. I can only see an Amitabh Bachchan, Shah Rukh Khan or Rajinikanth eliciting this kind of fervour among the public. Not that the crowds were small elsewhere in the country. He would be mobbed and his car followed in Delhi too.

Till the last week of his life, he was doing this. He was in Madurai about a week before his death in July 2015. He was so tired that day that he could not even stand up properly; still he kept meeting people. To garner this kind of response from people, he had to relentlessly project energy on his part. That must have sapped him. I feel he never allowed himself to rest and relax. He might have been in good health for a very long time had he kept a disciplined routine; after all, his older brother died a centenarian.

Kalam cared very much about how effective he was onstage or among people. Our job was also to observe how the audience responded. As President, after every programme, he would come to the working room and ask, 'How was my speech today, how was the response?' We had to tell him in an impartial way how we felt after listening to the speech and how the audience reacted. Sometimes his addresses could turn out to be duds and people would nod off. So we would have to tell him that too. Not tell, really, rather indicate. But always he expected us to say 'it was a hit'. Most of the time it was, but not always.

After November 2013, when he had a mild stroke, the slowing down began and he stopped asking us how his speeches had gone. Earlier, he would skip all the prepared stuff and launch straight into the subject. Sometimes he would talk at a very high pitch, then suddenly drop his tone. Up to 2008–2009, though he had the full text of his speech with him (and we a copy by the side), once he was seized by the energy of the moment, he would go extempore. It depended on the crowd and their response. From 2010–2011, we started using teleprompters at all the venues for his convenience and to avoid wastage of paper. Our teleprompters were relatively crude. We had the speech on our laptops and another would be in front of the lectern. You had to be alert every time he went extempore to keep track of where he last was so he could come back to his presentation. But he never pulled us up for any mistakes we made. He was sharp enough to manage, but would tell us later, 'You should not have shown me that page ...'

This sharpness declined after 2013. He did have small ups and downs earlier, mostly related to his fluctuating sugar levels, but those could be managed with small doses of medicine. Following his fall in his room in November 2013, his doctors said he had suffered a mild stroke. After that his movements and responses slowed. He would sit down slowly, get up slowly. Though he did not tell us to, we started pruning his programme itineraries. He would say, let's do this, this, this. And I would say, nothing doing, only two programmes. It was usual for us to have ten invitations from, say, Chandigarh or Bangalore in a month, but we would accept only two invitations.

We could not tell anyone that we were refusing the invites on account of Kalam's poor health, as he was dead against that. People began to think his staff were being arrogant. And Kalam himself never let on that he was tired, or not in the best of health, so they could not make out that he was not quite what he used to be. 'He is coming to our city/town, so why can he not visit our institution too?' we would be asked. We would have to give some excuse or the other. The talk was that 'the fellows in Kalam's office had to be coaxed' for his visits to be approved.

Kalam had overworked his staff, of course, but whenever we were in trouble he was exceedingly caring. When it occurred to him that he could do something for us, he would leave no stone unturned to help us. One morning in 2003 he told me, 'Why don't you bring your family to Rashtrapati Bhavan? Bring your parents over. After our tenure here, you won't be able to do that.'

I told him my father was suffering from Parkinson's disease. Immediately he said, 'For Parkinson's you have the best solution in Kerala. Take him to Kottakkal. There is no other medicine for the disease.' I told him my father was already under modern medication.

Kalam insisted that I ask my parents to visit and they did. They stayed with me in the President's Estate. Kalam granted us time on a Sunday. At 7.30 p.m., I took them to the President's room. To my parents he said, 'I have visited Palakkad many times. I don't go these days. I have a friend in Palakkad. He is called Prasad.' His words fell on me like a golden cloak, an accolade of a lifetime.

We sat for tea with the President and spent some time with him. After a few weeks' stay with us, my parents went back. Thereafter, my father's health deteriorated swiftly. Gradually, he became bedridden. I tried to take as much time as I could away from my work to be with him.

In 2004 and 2005, my father was in a very bad state. I used to receive frequent phone calls about his ill health. Once I was travelling by helicopter with President Kalam when one such call came, informing me that my father was seriously ill. They were planning to take him to a multi-speciality hospital in Coimbatore, which is not very far away from my home in Palakkad. So I spoke with Dr G. Bakthavathsalam, chairman of KG Hospitals, from the helicopter just as we were preparing for take-off, and explained to him my inability to reach Coimbatore. I requested his help in getting my father admitted as they were on their way to KG Hospital. Kind-hearted and compassionate, Dr Bakthavathsalam agreed to extend all possible assistance and also advised me to take care of the President and go ahead with my work. By the time I reached my destination my father had been admitted and emergency treatment had started. After a few days I managed to go to Coimbatore and be at my father's side for a few days. I thanked Dr Bakthavathsalam for his generosity and care. He told me openly, 'I have no extra commitment towards you. But I know that you are serving President Kalam. It is rare to have such a President. So I thought I should offer you whatever possible help from my side.' These words made my heart brim over with pride and gratitude. I let him know that I was honoured by his words.

After that, whenever my father had to be hospitalized, Dr Bakthavathsalam readily extended a helping hand. Once my family was running helter-skelter in search of an ambulance to take my father to hospital. My sister called me frantically and I had no other option but to call Dr Bakthavathsalam, who reassured me and sent his hospital ambulance to pick up my father from Palakkad and take him to his hospital in Coimbatore. This magnanimous doctor, out of his steadfast admiration for Kalam, did not even charge us for certain services. Though I tried to persuade him to accept payment, he repeatedly declined my offer.

In July 2007, three weeks before Kalam was to demit office, my father fell critically ill and I had to go and be with him. I went to the President and told him, 'Sir, my father is critically ill. He is slowly losing his memory. Tomorrow I have to go to Coimbatore and spend a few days with him. I want leave.' Since his demitting office was imminent, there was essential and urgent winding-up work to be completed, and I was sure the President would decline me leave. But to my surprise he immediately signed my leave application. 'OK. You go. Go and look after your father,' he said.

After finishing my work for the day and handing over the keys to the concerned staff, I was leaving office when my mobile phone rang. It was a call from 'The President' (that's the name under which I had saved his number). I had to leave early the next morning. I wondered why the President was calling me. I answered the call and heard his voice: 'What time are you going tomorrow?'

'Sir, 5 a.m. is my flight.'

'OK. Send that hospital number to my office and ask them to connect me to the hospital tomorrow morning, OK?'

'I will, sir,' I replied. I shared Dr Bakthavathsalam's number with the office and instructed the telephone exchange to connect the number to the President next morning at nine thirty.

When I reached the hospital, Dr Bakthavathsalam was standing in the portico. On seeing me he said, 'Welcome, Mr Prasad. See, the President of India has called me and requested me to take care of your father. Now tell me, what shall I do?' I was totally stumped. At a time when Rashtrapati Bhavan was fully engaged in the work of a President's demitting office, how could the President himself spare the time to talk to a doctor regarding the treatment of a staff member's parent? I told him, 'You don't have to do anything more than offering my father a comfortable room and good treatment. Because that's all we can do for a Parkinson's patient.' Dr Bakthavathsalam said, 'Don't worry, you just spend time with your father.' I was with my father for about a week. Slowly, his condition started improving. He was able to talk. I was happy and gratified. Soon, I left for Delhi and became immersed in office work again.

It was only because of Kalam's compassion that I could be with my father when he most needed me. I felt my presence was one reason he recovered so quickly. I should thank my family for looking after my father to the best of their abilities, especially my sister, who even took leave without pay to be with him. She never demanded my presence. Even when my father insisted on calling me from Delhi she advised him not to bother me. She recognized the importance of the office in which I worked and the person I was serving.

By the time my father breathed his last, Kalam was no longer president. In fact, he was away in the US at the time. Learning of my father's demise, he called to condole with me. On his return, he came to my office room and asked, 'Were you with your father at the time of death?' 'Yes, sir. I was.' Then, to console me, he said, 'What to do. People come and go. Life is like that.'

My father passed away in the early hours of 19 October 2007 at KG Hospital in my presence. Usually, private hospitals release the body only after all the bills have been settled. So we were prepared to wait until daybreak for the staff to come and process the papers. I was walking down the hospital stairs at 3 a.m. to arrange for a vehicle and settle the bill when to my utter surprise I found Dr Bakthavathsalam standing at the foot of the stairs waiting for me to clear the papers. He said, 'Come, Mr Prasad. I knew that your father is no more. That is why I came to the hospital immediately. Don't worry, you can take the body and leave right now. I have arranged for the hospital ambulance.' Again, I encountered exceptional goodness of heart! I could do nothing but bow before the generosity of the kind-hearted doctor.

To come back to Kalam's health, the former president did not take care of his health. For him, his energy came from his work and not from food. During his presidency, he could have had any kind of food for the asking, what with a battalion of cooks and attendants at his beck and call, but he never troubled them with requests for variety in his food. Sometimes he would wake up at 6 a.m., have a cup of tea and after a shower sit over a speech at 8.30 a.m. Naturally, some of us would be sitting with him. He would keep editing and tweaking the speech, frequently asking for tea and biscuits. The speech could perhaps take till 11.30 a.m. to be finalized, and he would have his breakfast only then. After breakfast he would call for a meeting that could go on till 4 p.m., after which he would have lunch. At 8 p.m. he often sat with a fresh bunch of papers and ended up having dinner close to midnight.

This kind of disorderliness in his lifestyle characterized every phase of his life.

Since he was a single man, we had to look after his health more closely than might otherwise have been the case. Perhaps he had been diabetic for some time, but the condition was diagnosed only during his presidency. He was on medication for it, but he was reluctant to talk about it with us. If he wanted to consult a doctor, he would have us call one, but would not tell us what difficulty he was experiencing. The doctor would come, examine him and usually prescribe some medicines. Kalam would instruct the doctor not to divulge any details about his health to us. But the doctors could not leave without keeping someone abreast of what was happening, as the President had no family around. Also, we were the people who had to buy his medicines and ensure that he had them on time.

His stroke in November 2013 and the unexpected demise of his friend Swaminathan that same year shook him quite a bit. He usually had a glass of milk before bedtime, which he would sip slowly. He would then go into his bedroom, informing us when he wanted his tea the next morning. That day, at the appointed time, the attendant brought his tea, kept it outside his room and knocked on the door, as usual, to indicate the tea was ready. He picked up the empty glass of milk from the night before. When he returned a little later, the tea was untouched. He replaced it with a fresh cup of tea, knocked on the door again, and left. Again, after an hour, he discovered the tea had not been touched.

The attendant called me, urging me to hurry. I knocked on Kalam's door and called out to him, 'Sir, please wake up.' There was his usual response, 'Yes, yes.' Another fresh cup of tea was placed on the table and we left. After an hour we came back to find the tea untouched. It was 10 a.m. Since this was very unusual behaviour for Kalam, I knocked forcefully on the door and said, 'Sir, we are going to break open the door.' That fetched the same reply: 'Yes, yes.' We broke open the door to see Kalam lying on the cold floor with froth coming out of his mouth. He was clad in a towel. We lifted him and laid him on the bed, cleaned him and simultaneously called for an ambulance to take him to the army hospital. The doctors diagnosed a slight haemorrhage. Sheridon and I were with him.

After a couple of days, we asked Kalam what exactly had happened. He recollected that he had woken up as usual at 6 a.m. and got up to switch on the lights. But he had pressed something else instead of the switch and had lost his grip on whatever it was and fallen down. It was a pity that he had had to lie on a cold floor for nearly five hours.

On the third day in the hospital, he had dysentery, probably because of the medicines. He could hardly get up from bed. On the sixth day, the doctors said he would have to stay there for one more week. A programme in Mumbai had to be cancelled. Kalam was extremely annoyed at this. He wanted to know what reason we had given the organizers. We told him, 'Sir, we have to tell them something close to the truth. We cannot lie outright to them. So we told them you are unwell and the programme had to be cancelled.'

'What problem did you say I have?' he snapped at us.

'Viral fever, common viral fever,' I said. He was happy to hear that.

A few more programmes were cancelled. During his hospital stay, he wanted to ensure that none of his family members visited him. They were panicking and wanted to come. But he told them he was doing all right and that they should not visit.

While he was being discharged, the doctors advised against frequent travel. So, no more hectic programmes for Kalam. When we conveyed the recommendations to him, he told us not to go by the doctors' words. 'Go by what I say, OK?'

He then asked us about his next programme. We told him all his programmes had been cancelled for one whole month. Looking back, I think his problem was not so much what people thought of his health as illness coming in the way of his travels and programmes. That was his life's passion; that is what energized him and kept him going.

Kalam's first programme after he recouped was in Chennai, in December. I was very anxious about his health. His walk was slightly wobbly and he seemed to have a memory problem too. After the fall, we had to explain things to him repeatedly. On the eve of the Chennai visit, I told him, 'Sir, tomorrow we are going to Chennai.'

'Chennai? For what?' We had to tell him many times why we were going before it registered in his mind. On such difficult days I had to keep checking with the household attendants to remind him about his schedule, his programme and the place of visit.

I had a particularly tense visit to Nagpur with him. We took an IndiGo flight, and as usual he was accorded a warm welcome, and many people lined up to get autographs from him. Everything seemed to be going well. When we reached the Nagpur guest house, he seemed to have forgotten where he had come and for what. In his room in the guest house, he began to ask me frantically, 'Is this my room? Where is my shirt? Where is my bag?' I panicked. Whatever had happened to Kalam! It took a couple of minutes for me to get a grip on the situation. Kalam believed he had reached his room in Delhi and that someone had taken away his belongings.

I looked him straight in the face and told him firmly, 'Sir, this is Nagpur. We have come here to attend an NIT programme. After the programme, we will go back to Delhi today. This is not your room. This is a guest house.'

'No, no,' he said. 'Take me to my room. Where is my room?'

The room attendant brought fresh coconut water. He drank it and sat down for a while. I stood nearby and watched him and, once more, in a low voice, told him everything that I had said earlier. It was as though he had regained awareness after a brief blackout. 'Oh, this is Nagpur? This is the guest house?'

I was in a room adjacent to his. It was the general practice that whoever accompanied him stayed in the room next to his. He had a habit of locking his room, but I cautioned him not to do so. I was also worried about what he might say when he met the vice chancellor and the team of organizers who had invited us. The slightest bit of memory loss on his part would have consequences. But the programme went very well and Kalam gave an impressive talk.

Early in 2015, we were in Bangalore, scheduled to depart the city at 10 a.m. Again, Kalam did not open the door. I got worried. Maybe he had fallen again. Afraid, I called an attendant and he forced open the door. Kalam was inside and was all right. He was taking an unusually long time to get ready due to his slow pace.

From December 2013 onward, we had been taking extra care of him and were extra vigilant at his programmes. No more than two programmes a day – even that was quite a lot – and he was not to lock his room from the inside. If there was a stretch of walking to do in the open, we would ensure someone went along in case he lost his balance and fell. I would also keep the window of my room open to keep a watch on him if he decided to step out into the veranda or compound. As we cut down the number of programmes, the number of invitations only increased. Soon it was again back to four programmes a day, wherever he travelled. All we could do was ensure he got adequate rest in between.

I became a tense person whenever I had to travel with him. Any delay on his part in coming out of his room at the scheduled hour would send shock waves through me. Initially, he kept his promise and didn't lock his room, but he began to lock it later, adding to our stress. Often I would anxiously knock on his door if he did not emerge from his room at the usual time. Fortunately, there weren't any untoward incidents after the 2013 episode. Gradually, things started settling down to a satisfactory routine.

9

The Last Trip

In July 2015, Kalam got a urinary infection. The doctor told me that there was pus in his urine. He assured me that the infection could be cured through proper medication, and sure enough, within a few days, Kalam regained normal health. When we were planning his Shillong visit, he had no noticeable health problem. But then, even if he had had any he would not have allowed us to cancel a programme that he had agreed to, especially one that required him to lecture IIM students. His lecture at IIM Shillong was slated for Monday, 27 July. I had asked Dhanshyam Sharma, additional personal secretary, to accompany him to Shillong. If on other days I reached office by 8.45 a.m., on Saturdays I would clock in only at around 11 a.m. The Saturday before his trip, as I entered the office, he buzzed me. I went to his room.

'Monday I have to visit Shillong,' he told me.

'Yes, sir.'

'What am I going to Shillong for?'

'Sir, you are going to take classes at IIM Shillong.'

'How is the weather there?'

'It is pleasant, sir. Between 20 and 21 degrees Celsius.'

'So I don't need to carry woollens?'

'No, you don't.'

In the afternoon he called me again and wanted my assistance should the young man who had been hired to help him with research and inputs for his talks not turn up to prepare his lecture for IIM Shillong. I agreed to help. In the meantime, the assistant turned up and sat with Kalam.

On Monday, when I reached office, the attendant asked me to call Kalam using the internal phone. Kalam had been pressing the buzzer 7 a.m. onward, I was told. I immediately called him.

'Sir, I hear you have been trying to reach me. What can I do for you?'

'Yes. I want to know the temperature in Shillong. Should I take my woollens?'

He is repeating the same question, I told myself.

'Sir, I checked the weather this morning. The temperature in Shillong is 21 degrees Celsius. There is a light drizzle there.'

'So no need for woollens?'

'No need to carry woollens.'

'Get me a printout of the weather report.'

I got him a printout.

At 10.30 a.m. he came to my office room and inquired if the family of Kurup, his former colleague at ISRO, had arrived. I informed him that Kurup's family was already in the guest room. He went to the guest room to chat with them. They were the last visitors he received. After they left, he came out of his office room at 11 a.m. He went to the toilet and got ready for his flight. I followed him up to the car. I closed the door after he got in, and unusually he wished me 'good luck'. That was not normal for him. 'Thank you, sir,' I said.

I was tracking their journey as was my usual practice and received the report of their safe landing in Guwahati. After lunch, they set off for Shillong by car. They reached Shillong at around 6 p.m. and had tea. That evening I was sitting outside my office when one of the attendants rushed to me with tears in his eyes. He said, 'Mr Sharma has been trying you for a long time. Please call him – something has happened to Sir.' Since he could not get me, he had alerted the attendant to get in touch with me. The attendant told me that Kalam had fallen from the stage.

I rushed to the office and called back Sharma. I asked Sharma if it was on account of vertigo. He said, 'No, sir, he is no more. The doctors said he is no more.' I was so shocked at this I stood there as if I had blacked out. It was a few seconds before I could come back to reality. I called our doctor and conveyed the message to him.

I wanted him to contact the doctor in Shillong and reconfirm everything. I felt dizzy. Seeing my condition, the doctor gave me a dose of tranquillizer to keep my blood pressure down. After a while, he confirmed the terrible news. I then contacted the PMO and conveyed the message to the prime minister's private secretary and I requested a helicopter for bringing the body to Delhi. He agreed to do everything and told me that his office had already been informed of the sad news. The PMO receives such news first, through the Intelligence Bureau circuit. By then the news started flashing in the media. My phone kept ringing. I was devastated, both physically and mentally. I was not in a frame of mind to talk to anyone other than my colleagues. I called Sheridon, who was away on leave, and conveyed the news and asked him to fly back that night.

Kalam had not fallen down from the stage, as the attendant had told me. He had collapsed onstage while giving his lecture. He had been taken to Bethany Hospital in the city, where he was declared brought dead. He had had a massive cardiac arrest and passed away onstage. He had always wished to have a sudden death.

The government machinery was set in motion. I had to help from the departed leader's office, which was in a way his family too. I was the lone man there, having to deal with queries from government authorities as to where the body should be kept, where it had to be taken for the public to pay their last respects and when. Then there were the many calls from various people and organizations.

His relatives in Rameswaram had not been informed. It fell on me to tell them. I got his niece Naseema on the phone and told her that her uncle was no more. She asked me where the body would be taken. His family discussed this among themselves, and his eldest brother, A.P.J. Maraikkayar, told me, 'You bring him here.' Meanwhile, the government was asking me to communicate our final decision about the venue for the last rites. I told them about the family's wishes. So it was ultimately decided to take Kalam's body to Rameswaram. I felt crushed with sorrow and exhaustion that night. I went to bed at 2 a.m. but I could only afford a short sleep and had to be up at 5 a.m.

In the morning, the body was flow from Guwahati to Delhi, where it lay in state the whole day. Hundreds of thousands of people, from commoners to dignitaries, came to pay their last respects to the great soul. On the morning of 29 July, the body was carried to Rameswaram by a military aircraft. We accompanied the body. By 4 p.m. we were in Rameswaram, where for the rest of the day the public were allowed to bid him goodbye. The following day the body was taken for the last rites.

A great soul had dissolved into the majestic history of our great nation. His words resound in our hearts and his precious messages to us linger in our minds. Both the rich and the poor carried Kalam in their hearts, I felt. They were touched by his passion for life, his energy and his clean-heartedness.

I was utterly desolate. For me his death was not merely the loss of a beloved boss. I felt personally bereaved. To me he was akin to close family. Those days were the start of a most dismal period for me. After my boss's death, the whole nation was extolling his virtues. Many organizations, institutions and individuals announced new or revamped projects dedicated to or citing Kalam's vision and goals. But I had no one to turn to when it came to a small desire of my own. With my position as private secretary to the former president having come to a close, I had to rejoin my parent department. Before that I wanted to ensure that at my new job I was given all the legitimate credit I was entitled to for the services I had provided as private secretary to Kalam, both as President and as former president. But due consideration for the work I had done was denied me by the office. I didn't lose hope. I decided to submit my case before the higher authorities.

After all, I had served the most righteous leader of the country. My boss hadn't pledged allegiance to any political party. He was a visionary whose heart had enough place to accommodate all good ideas and views, regardless of which party professed them. I was very confident that if not my officers, their superiors would lend me an ear and approve my request. I decided to first contact the private secretary to the prime minister, who then was doing the same kind of service that I had performed for Kalam both during and after his presidency. I was sure he would consider my request and assign me appropriate weightage for the work I had done for Kalam all these years. I got him on the telephone. He listened to me for ten minutes and simply hung up on me.

But I had been with the indefatigable Kalam all these years. I thought I would get justice from a senior officer in the PMO. I called many times, seeking an appointment to meet him and to explain my situation. The first two calls were politely reciprocated, but no appointment was granted. My third call was attended to by one of the officer's staff, who sounded as though he was speaking on the instructions of someone behind him. When I mentioned Kalam, the person acted ignorant and said, 'Who is he?'

Next, I approached Sadananda Gowda, minister for programme implementation, who had been a good friend of Kalam's. Whenever Kalam visited Bangalore when Gowda was chief minister of Karnataka, the latter would call on Kalam as a courtesy. I hoped he would be more generous to me than those I had talked to so far. He listened to me and was very sympathetic. He took up my submission when he was going for a meeting at the PMO but was much dejected when the PMO summarily rejected the petition. Kalam was no more and I was small fry, a small cog in the giant wheel of the government. I wondered what the fuss was all about in denying me such a small request for something that was actually deserved.

I didn't want to end my struggle for justice. I kept on trying to meet various other people who I thought would be of help. After a year and a half, I tried to meet the then national president of the BJP. His office reciprocated my call cordially and included my name in an appointment list for the party president. One day the office of the party president called and they connected me to him. I briefly explained my representation to him. He heard me out patiently and said he would give me time later on a suitable day. Days and weeks passed. I got no word from the office. When I checked with the office, I was told that my name was put on the list, but was struck out from the day's appointments. I continued to pursue my case with members of Parliament. Subramanian Swamy of the BJP and Shashi Tharoor of the Congress were both sympathetic towards me, but could not do anything. 'You know my standing with the people in power. If I take up your case, it will be rejected then and there,' said Tharoor.

I felt sad that after the life of honesty and dedication that Kalam had lived, few in power held him in any esteem. All those high words upon his demise were mere lip service. Political leaders, after all, simply want loyalty. Kalam never kow-towed to anyone in politics. He never sought patronage, never ran after political bigwigs to secure a second term, even though he was prodded to do so. The people of India may have him in their hearts, but not so its leaders.

If this is the case with a great soul called Dr A.P.J. Abdul Kalam, then what chance do lesser mortals have?

I wandered through miles of government office corridors seeking approval for what I thought was my very modest demand. I will never forget my meeting with a senior minister. Without a trace of courtesy, and without even gesturing to me to sit, he said, 'So you have worked with Kalam for so many years! Who told you to serve Kalam? We didn't tell you. Nothing is possible in your case.'

'Sir, please help me,' I pleaded with him. He replied dismissively, 'No, nothing can be done for you.' One of his officers took on from there and said in a mocking tone, 'Who is this Kalam, yaar?'

I came away with a heavy heart. Kalam's life had hardly been rosy. He had received bouquets and brickbats in good measure. There had been people who humiliated him, people who used his name to get ahead. But Kalam never exacted revenge on them, or even spoke ill of them. I had never heard him make a single scornful or judgemental comment about anybody. His strongest expression of frustration with someone was to refer to the person as '*funny guy*'. That was the harshest phrase that could come from Kalam. Even when I had slipped up at work occasionally, Kalam would use the same phrase for me. That this was his strongest expression of rage or scorn was telling of how decent and innocent a human being he was. In fact, I wanted to title this book 'Kalam and His Funny Guys'.

All those who humiliated me for the small favour I asked of them, I called them 'funny guys' in my mind and cast them aside. That is what my sweet-natured boss had taught me.

Had he been alive today and seen me rushing about with my request, he would have called up someone in authority and said, 'One of my guys has a modest request ...'

Appendix

Address to the Parliament: Farewell Function Hosted by the Speaker Lok Sabha at the Central Hall of Parliament House, New Delhi

'Vision for the nation emanates from Parliament'

Honourable Members of Parliament, my greetings to all of you. It has been a great experience for me working with the members of Parliament during the last five years. I have addressed the Parliament ten times; I have had the benefit of interacting with you at individual and specialist's group levels. I thank every one of you for your cooperation.

During my period of presidency, two governments have been in place and both the Prime Ministers, Shri Atal Bihari Vajpayee and Dr Manmohan Singh, have had many meetings with me and I have had the fortune and benefit of their counsel. The Presiding Officers of Lok Sabha and Rajya Sabha have the important mission of catalysing the best performance of the parliament. I would like to congratulate the Speaker of the Lok Sabha, Shri Somnath Chatterjee, for his efforts to create a high-tech museum depicting the continuum of democratic heritage in India. Also his efforts in creating Lok Sabha TV for televising the proceedings are in line with the needs of modern democracy. Our former Vice President Bhairon Singh Shekhawat, a remarkable person with a wide canvass of experience, has received general appreciation from all about the way in which he conducted the Rajya Sabha proceedings. I also enjoyed working with him as a Vice President. I congratulate the President-elect Smt. Pratibha Patil on this historic occasion and wish her all the best in her mission.

On this occasion, I would like to recollect with appreciation the contributions made by the past Presidents of India, each one bringing his own core competence to the Rashtrapati Bhavan. I would like to thank the Governors and Lt. Governors of all the states and union territories and the Chief Ministers of all the states for their cooperation, when I visited the states and union territories. Particularly, I would like to thank the Chief Ministers and the Presiding Officers of the Legislative Assemblies of fourteen states and union territories for facilitating me to share the vision for their states and the missions thereon.

Dear Parliament members, I realize and appreciate how Parliamentary debates and decisions have led the nation today towards an ascending economic trajectory. Nation's standing in the world is clearly visible. I have witnessed this special aspect during my visits to sixteen countries. As the President of India, I had the privilege to address various parliaments abroad including the European Union Parliament. I am happy to note that the special respect for Indians during my interactions with many heads of states and delegations visiting India.

Distinctive Profile of India 2020

With this background, I visualize the following distinctive profile of India by the year 2020.

1. A Nation where the rural and urban divide has reduced to a thin line.
2. A Nation where there is an equitable distribution and adequate access to energy and quality water.
3. A Nation where agriculture, industry and service sector work together in symphony.
4. A Nation where education with value system is not denied to any meritorious candidates because of societal or economic discrimination.
5. A Nation which is the best destination for the most talented scholars, scientists and investors.
6. A Nation where the best of healthcare is available to all.
7. A Nation where the governance is responsive, transparent and corruption free.
8. A Nation where poverty has been totally eradicated, illiteracy removed and crimes against women and

children are absent and none in the society feels alienated.

9. A Nation that is prosperous, healthy, secure, devoid of terrorism, peaceful and happy and continues with a sustainable growth path.
10. A Nation that is one of the best places to live in and is proud of its leadership through creative and effective leadership in Parliament, State Assemblies and other institutions of the state.

Integrated Action for Developed India

To achieve the distinctive profile of India, all of us have before us the mission of transforming India into a developed nation. In order to succeed in our mission, the key five areas where India has a core competence for integrated action are: (1) Agriculture and Food Processing, (2) Education and Healthcare, (3) Infrastructure: Reliable and quality electric power, surface transport and infrastructure for all parts of the country, (4) Information and Communication Technology, and (5) Self-Reliance in Critical Technologies.

These five areas are closely inter-related and, if progressed in a coordinated way, will lead to food, economic and national security. One of the major missions within these five areas is the development of infrastructure for bringing rural prosperity through

Provision of Urban Amenities in Rural Areas (PURA) by creating three connectivities namely physical, electronic and knowledge, leading to economic connectivity. The number of PURA clusters for the whole country is estimated to be 7,000. Simultaneously, from energy and environmental considerations, we should aim at achieving Energy Independence by 2030. Energy independence has got to be achieved through three different sources namely renewable energy (solar, wind and hydro power), electrical power from nuclear energy and biofuel for the transportation sector. Energy independence throws very important technological challenges to the country.

While we are happy that our economy is in the ascent phase and our GDP is growing at nearly 9 per cent per annum, it is evident that economic growth is not fully reflected in the quality of life of a large number of people, particularly in rural areas and even in urban areas. Hence, we have evolved what is called a 'National Prosperity Index (NPI)' which is a summation of (a) annual growth rate of GDP; plus (b) improvement in quality of life of the people, particularly those living below the poverty line; plus (c) the adoption of a value system derived from our civilizational heritage in every walk of life which is unique to India. That is NPI=a+b+c. Particularly, 'b' is a function of availability of housing, good water, nutrition, proper sanitation, quality education, quality healthcare and employment potential; 'c' is a function of promoting the joint family system, creation of a spirit of working together, leading a righteous way of life, removing social inequities and above all promoting a conflict-free, harmonious society. This will be indicated by peace in families and communities, reduction in corruption index, reduction in court cases, elimination of violence against children and women and communal tensions. There should be progressive reduction in the number of people living below the poverty line leading to its becoming near zero by 2020. All our efforts in improving the national economic performance should be guided by the measured NPI of the nation at any point of time.

How shall we realize this vision? What are the immediate steps that we need to take to realize this vision?

My interaction with many of you and my understanding of the various central and state programmes, the initiatives of private and non-governmental organizations as well as the overwhelming desire of citizens to participate in the national development gives me the confidence that our society is ready to work for these missions. May I suggest that you all work together to evolve two major initiatives:

1. To formulate an Energy Independence Bill – A three-dimensional approach for energy choice towards realizing clean planet earth.
2. To adopt a resolution for Vision 2020: Adopt a resolution that India will be transformed into a safe, prosperous, happy and socioeconomically developed nation before the year 2020 using NPI as a measure.

You will agree with me the importance of making these bills a reality in a time-bound manner.

Challenges before Parliament of the 21st Century

I have narrated the profile of the nation by 2020 and the actions needed to achieve the missions. While we have made significant gains in our economic performance, our performance on a range of human development and governance indicators require significant improvement to achieve the status of a fully developed nation. The future political leadership the world over has to rise to the challenge of sustainability of growth, development, environment and resources. Honourable members, you have a major role to play in the creation of future leadership for the 21st century in creating missionary zeal among the youth of the nation to promote moral strength, security and prosperity for our people.

Parliamentary Vision for the Nation

At the dawn of the 21st century, Parliament, like any other institution, faces greater challenges than ever before, especially on matters related to human development and governance. India can be rightly proud of its leadership and its many achievements in economic, social, scientific and political fields over the past 60 years. But we cannot afford to rest content with the past achievements and we have to march in tune with the challenges of 21st century in technology, industry, agriculture, trade, governance system and leadership style. National leadership has to radiate confidence in our people that 'we can do it'.

The challenges in realizing the developed India vision 2020 provide also opportunities for innovation in every aspect of governance and legislative actions. As we review the governance system and legislative processes for the 21st century, full advantages and implications of technological revolutions, national and global connectivities, globalization and international cooperation and competition have to be taken into account.

Conclusion

Honourable Members of Parliament may like to debate these suggestions and evolve, with unified and harmonious leadership, a Parliamentary Vision for the

Nation, in the same manner as when our Constitution was first drawn up. This 21st Century Parliamentary Vision for India needs to have a global and long-term perspective, and needs to be underpinned with implementation strategies, integrated structures and action plans for transforming India into a developed country by 2020 with NPI as a measure and acquire energy independence before 2030.

It is this unique Parliamentary Vision and its effective implementation that would make our billion people smile and smile together. Working together in unity and harmony for a national vision is the greatest need of the hour for our parliamentarians. You will agree with me that this is one of the most important missions of our Parliament today.

May I once again convey my gratitude to all the Honourable Members of Parliament and my best wishes to all of you in your mission of realizing the goals of developed India 2020.

May God bless you.

Acknowledgements

I thank Shri Pratap Nair and Shri Sivakumar for encouraging and convincing me when I was reluctant to write. Without Shri Pratap Nair's support this book would not have taken shape. My deep respects and regards to him. I also thank Krishan Chopra for readily agreeing to publish the book and for his constant encouragement. I thank Kripa Raman and Jaishree Ram Mohan for help with getting the words right. I thank R. Sivapriya for her valuable advice and support right from the beginning. Finally, I thank my family for their continued support though they worry about repercussions.

Index

About the Author

R.K. Prasad was A.P.J. Abdul Kalam's private secretary. He served Kalam for over two decades, from 1993 at the ministry of defence and later as part of the President's staff, until his death in 2015. Prasad now works in an organisation under the Ministry of Defence.